Funny Bones

Funny Bones

Comedy Games and Activities for Kids

Lisa Bany-Winters

CHICAGO REVIEW PRESS

Library of Congress Cataloging-in-Publication Data
Bany-Winters, Lisa
    Funny bones: comedy games and activities for kids / Lisa Bany-Winters.
        p. cm.
    Includes bibliographical references and index.
    Summary: Provides information on how to be funny, including ideas about
comedic styles and routines, how to use props, developing a distinctive character,
using music, improvisational techniques, as well as the history of comedy and some
well-known people in the field.
    ISBN: 1-55652-444-7
    1. Games—Juvenile literature. 2. Amusement—Juvenile literature. 3. Creative activities
and seat work—Juvenile literature. [1. Comedy. 2. Amusements. 3. Games.]   I. Title.

GV1203 .B317 2002
793—dc21

                                                                                2001052477

The author and the publisher disclaim all liability for use of the information
contained in this book.

Cover design and illustration: Fran Lee
Interior design and illustration: Rattray Design

Published by Chicago Review Press, Incorporated
814 North Franklin Street
Chicago, Illinois 60610
ISBN 1-55652-444-7
Printed in the United States of America
5 4 3 2

To my family
And everyone who laughs with us
In loving memory of Skylar Nicole Baney

Contents

Foreword

"Laughter is the shortest distance between two people."

—Victor Borge

A straight line may be the shortest distance between two points, but laughter is surely the shortest distance between people. Nobody seems to understand this truth better than Lisa Bany-Winters. Having thoroughly enjoyed her first two books, *Show Time!* and *On Stage* (how wise that the judges at the Parent's Choice Association were to confer their Approval Seal for Excellence on her delightful *On Stage: Theater Games and Activities for Kids*), I was eagerly awaiting her workshop at a professional conference in the fall of 2001. The room was filled with teachers, directors, librarians, social workers, actors, recreation leaders—good-hearted people one and all hoping to make a difference in the lives of children. But the atmosphere in the room before the workshop started was hushed and, well, awkward. Participants sat stiffly in their chairs. The room was polite and quiet and reserved. Then Lisa Bany-Winters entered. Everything changed. In moments, the room was filled with laughter. We were up and on our feet and Lisa was guiding us through an exercise and everyone was laughing. The workshop flew by, with participants commenting, "I can't remember when I've laughed so hard while learning so much." It was clear to all of us that we were in the presence of a very gifted teacher who loves what she is doing. When I complimented her afterward on the exceptional work, she said simply, "I had a good time, too. My husband teases that I do this work so I will always have someone to play with me." If I had a magic wand, I would love to make it possible for everybody who wants to bring light into the lives of children to take a class with Lisa. But she has given us something better than a magic wand; Lisa has given us a wonderful resource in the form of *Funny Bones: Comedy Games and Activities for Kids.*

Neil Postman warned us of the consequences for a society that compels its children to grow up too quickly in his groundbreaking work *The Disappearance of Childhood.* I can't think of a better way to help children stay children than by giving them the gift of laughter. As British poet Margaret Slackville once wrote, "Laughter is ever young!" In *Funny Bones*, Lisa has assembled a marvelous array of exercises, games, songs, and scenes designed to keep us all forever young. How can you take yourself too seriously when singing "Waddily Acha"? What better remedy for the blues than a round of "Boppity Boppity Bop"? And just try thinking Shakespeare is stuffy and boring after exploring the excerpt from *Twelfth Night*! In the words of Theodore Geisel (Dr. Seuss), "I like nonsense, it wakes up the brain cells. Fantasy is a necessary ingredient in living."

Humorist Bennett Cerf once wrote, "A person who can bring the spirit of laughter into a room is indeed blessed." Clearly, Lisa Bany-Winters has been blessed with this gift. How fortunate for teachers and youth leaders and camp counselors and drama directors that she has chosen to share her gift with all of us in this well-written, user-friendly resource book. *Funny Bones* will make a welcome addition to many a library, empowering adults to help children experience the richness and joy of comedy. Few gifts could be more valuable; perhaps as we face the future we would do well to heed the advice of Mark Twain and "Laugh until our cheeks hurt! The human race has one really effective weapon, and that is laughter."

—Rives B. Collins, Northwestern University
Department of Theatre Head, Theatre
for Young Audiences

Acknowledgments

I am indebted to the following people and organizations: Stephanie and Joe Albright, Josh Andrews, Arnold Aprill, Bree Baney, Martin Bany, Nancy and John Bany, Megan Baskin, Brian Boller, Margo Chervony, Chicago Arts Partnerships in Education, Geoff Coates, Martin de Maat, Drama Disciples, Jayme Ernsteen, Paul Finnigan, Bryce Friedman, Richard Friedman, Melanie Gordon, Barbara Heaton, B. J. Jones, Michele Klemm, Jason Lubow, Dan Macsai, Dana and Anthony McKinney, Emily McNish, Mari Meyer, Emily Mott, Northlight Improv Comedy Kids, Northlight Kids Players, Northlight Teen Players, Sheldon Patinkin, Darlene Pearlstein, Jerry Proffit, Danny Robles, J. R. Rose, Rebecca Rubenstein, Philip Schuster, Mara Silver, Neal Simons, Cheryl Sloane, Joyce Sloane, St. Athanasius Roman Catholic Church in Evanston, Amy Weiss, Brian Winters, and Gavin Witt.

The following people were coadapters of the plays included in this book (character names are in parentheses). All plays were originally directed by me for Emanon Theater Company. For *Sally Ann Thunder Ann Whirlwind* I'd like to thank Barbara Kanady (Sally), Chas Vrba (Pa, Mike, and Davey), Marcy Konlon (Ma and Bear), and Joe Albright (Lucy and Tree). For *Alice in Wonderland* (both the tea party and court scenes), adapted from the book by Lewis Carroll, I'd like to thank Stephanie Repin (Alice), Joe Albright (White Rabbit), Danny Robles (Caterpillar and Cook), Ed Nishioka (Cheshire Cat), Geoff Coates (Duchess and Dormouse), Brian Winters (Mad Hatter),

Anthony McKinney (March Hare), and Klahr Thorsen (Queen of Hearts). For *Rapunzel*, adapted from the story by the Brothers Grimm, I'd like to thank Amy Harmon (Demon Radish/Bird), Julie Lockhart (Witch), Janet Tuegel (Rapunzel/Rapunzel's Mother), Ashley Hugen (Bingo/Rapunzel's Father), and Joe Albright (Prince/Ogre). For *Jemima Puddle Duck*, adapted from the book by Beatrix Potter, Danny Robles (Jemima), Joe Albright (Fox), Stephanie Repin (Farm Dog), Geoff Coates (Narrator/Ensemble), and Laura Holliday, Laura Pruden, and Rick Schnier (Ensemble).

A very special thanks to Barbara Kanady and Brad Larsen, who have taught, learned, and laughed alongside me, and to Northlight Theatre for providing the creative playing field.

Introduction

When my daughter was two years old she dumped her cup of apple juice on her head one day at preschool. When I asked her why she did that, she said, "Because it was funny." It was difficult to argue with her reasoning. Later that same year she told me, "Mommy, it's funny when I sing "Ding Dong the Witch Is Dead" with my tongue out." She showed me, and I had to agree it was indeed funny. I have seen firsthand a child discovering humor.

Dr. Patch Adams strongly believes that humor and laughter are healing to humans. He founded the Gesundheit! Institute where he practices the belief that fun, friendship, and joy are important parts of health care, and that fun and laughter are medicine. Many children develop self-confidence and overcome shyness when they realize they can be funny. This book is designed to bring out the humor in all young people, and will give them a lot of ideas for having fun and being funny. You don't need to know jokes to make people laugh. This book is full of ideas for creating your own comic routines and comedy scenes.

Here's the fun and funny you'll find as you turn these pages. In Chapter 1 you'll find information on famous comics and ideas for creating your own comedic style and trademark. Chapter 2 will get you started with ideas for creating original comic material. The history of comedy, along with activities that illustrate some of the elements of humor found in historical comedies, is included. Chapter 3 takes you a step further by helping you make your comic material as funny as it can be. Chapter 4 explores how props can be used in comedy. Sometimes even the most ordinary everyday object can lead to humor. Many comics become other people in their comedy routines. Chapter 5 contains character activities and games so you can become anyone you wish. You can use music in your comedy. In addition to acting silly, you can also sing and dance in silly ways. Chapter 6 has funny songs and ideas for hilarious dances you can do. Improvisation is a popular form of comic acting. Chapter 7 explores improv techniques and the self-confidence exercises needed to perform comedy, while Chapter 8 contains improv games and scene ideas to hone those skills. You might see these improv games at an improv comedy club or on the television show called *Whose Line Is It, Anyway?* Nonsense words and sounds are a source of humor for people from infancy on. Chapter 9 is filled with games and activities that bring out the silly sounds and words in you. And while I do not suggest dumping your cup of juice on your head as my daughter did, you will find a lot of suggestions for physical comedy that you can do in Chapter 10. When you have a group of people, such as at a party or in a classroom, you can sit or stand in a circle and play the humorous games found in Chapter 11. Chapter 12 includes funny scenes for you to act out. Along the way you'll find ways to have even more fun whenever you see "More Laughs" for activity variations. You'll also find interesting sidebars throughout, and in the back of the book there are suggestions for more funny plays, comedic resources, and a glossary of comedy terms.

Ready, set, make 'em laugh!

Funny Bones

Making People Laugh

Stand-up comedy is a humorous performance by a solo artist or sometimes teams of artists also known as *comics*. Sometimes stand-up routines are made up of jokes and one-liners, and funny stories and situations, or they revolve around humorous characters created by the performer. Many actors such as Whoopi Goldberg, Jerry Seinfeld, Rosie O'Donnell, and Eddie Murphy got their start doing stand-up comedy.

If someone is laughing, something is funny, but why and how? This chapter will explore some famous comics and what makes them so funny. The Marx Brothers, Charlie Chaplin, Lily Tomlin, and Eddie Murphy are comics with vastly different styles, but they all have one thing in common: they are very funny. There are games and activities to help you explore different styles and discover how comics develop their style. Throughout these activities you can think about your own personal style, and see how it develops in different humorous ways.

Meet the Marx Brothers

The Marx Brothers were a comedy team of five brothers all born in New York City in the late 1800s to early 1900s. They were the sons of German immigrants. Their mother, Minnie Marx, was a famous stage mother because she pushed her sons to become performers. Comedy was in her blood as well. She performed in vaudeville with her brother Al Shean in a duo called Gallagher. The five Marx Brothers performed comedy routines, but it was three of them—Groucho, Harpo, and Chico—who became most successful starring in a number of movies. The musical play *Minnie's Boys* tells their life story both on and off the stage. See if you can figure out how the brothers came up with their stage names.

Stage Names	Real Names
Groucho	Julius
Harpo	Adolph
Chico	Leonard
Gummo	Milton
Zeppo	Herbert

Julius was often a grouchy person, so his nickname was Groucho. Adolph played the harp, and Milton liked to chew gum. Think of things you like or things about yourself. See if you can make up a funny name for yourself by adding an *O* to these words. For example, if you play the drums, your nickname could be Drummo. If you like to play sports, you could be Sporto. If you love to drink soda pop, you could be Poppo. Imagine what kind of comedic character would have these names.

Who's on First?

Abbott and Costello were comedy film partners. They were born William A. Abbott and Louis Francis Cristillo. Both had experience as actors before teaming up for films. Costello always played the clown or silly role, and Abbott always played the *straight man*, or the serious one in their routines. They began performing on the radio together in 1938. The next year they appeared on Broadway, and after that they went on to make a number of successful films. Their first film was *Buck Privates* in 1941.

One of Abbott and Costello's comic routines involved miscommunication and some people with very unusual names.

Abbott tries to explain to Costello the names of the players on a baseball team.

Abbott says, "Who's on first, What's on second and I Don't Know's on third base."

Costello becomes confused and asks, "Who's on first?"

"That's right," says Abbott, "and What's on second."

Costello thinks Abbott asked him a question, and replies, "I don't know!"

Abbot replies, "He's on third."

The conversation continues with much humor as Costello gets more and more confused!

Create your own confusing conversation by using silly names. Here are some examples.

- Pretend you have a dog named Stay. Try calling him by saying, "Come here, Stay!"
- Pretend you're casting a play with Who, What, and I Don't Know Who. Who's Romeo, What's Juliet, and I Don't Know Who's the nurse.
- Pretend your parents' names are Sleepy and Grumpy. Try telling your friend, "My mom's Sleepy and my Dad's Grumpy."
- Pretend your friends are named Red, Yellow, and Blue. Explain playing Twister with these friends.

Create a Trademark Character

One or more players

Charlie Chaplin was an actor, producer, screen-writer, director, and composer! He was born in London, and both of his parents were music hall entertainers. He started out by touring England in a children's musical company called Eight Lancashire Lads. This led him to roles as an actor. When he was 17 he joined a revue that toured the United States. There, in 1913, a film producer hired him. His first film was called *Making a Living*, but it was in his film *Kid Auto Races* that he created the character that is his trademark. He named the character the Little Tramp. The highly recognizable character wore a bowler hat, baggy pants, and shoes that were too big, and he walked with a cane.

You can create your own trademark character.

Props

A number of unusual clothing items and objects

Choose at least three things to wear or hold, such as an ugly tie, sunglasses, and a banana. Create a character around these things. Think about what kind of person would wear an ugly tie and sunglasses and carry around a banana. Exaggerate your actions to create your character. Practice how the character walks and talks. Practice talking like the character to other people. See how many characters you can create.

Little Child in a Big Chair

One or more players

ily Tomlin is a comic who was born in Detroit, Michigan. She first became successful in 1969 on a television show called *Laugh In*. She is best known for her funny, unusual characters. She put many of her characters in her one-woman show called *The Search for Signs of Intelligent Life in the Universe*, which won a Tony Award in 1985. She reprised the role in the year 2000.

One of her famous characters was a little girl. She made herself look small for the role by sitting in a giant rocking chair. Because the chair was so big, she looked like a little girl sitting in it, even though she was a grown-up.

The character of the little girl was based on real children. Small children, who don't completely understand grown-ups and are still learning how to speak properly, often say very funny things on purpose or by accident.

If you have little brothers or sisters, talk to them. Ask them to tell you a story, or just ask them about their day. If you don't have any younger siblings, see if you can talk to a younger neighbor or a friend's younger brothers or sisters. As they speak, listen closely to the sound of their voices, and watch how they sit and move.

Make a giant, oversized chair out of boxes or pillows. Sit in your chair, and retell some of the stories a younger child told you. Mimic the child's voice and movements.

At the end of her child routine, Tomlin would say, "And that's the truth," and she would blow a raspberry by sticking her tongue out and forcing air out to make her lips vibrate and make a sound. See if you can think of a funny way to end your stories.

Impressions

ha ha

Mimicking is different from impressions. To *mimic* means to act out or become another person like the child in the previous exercise. The character activities in Chapter 5 will help you in your mimicking. Doing impressions is similar to mimicking, only the person you are doing an impression of is a celebrity or someone very recognizable.

Eddie Murphy was born in Brooklyn, New York. He watched a lot of television growing up, and learned to do impressions of his favorite cartoon characters. When he was 15 years old he hosted a talent show. He did some of his impressions in the show and was a big hit. By high school he knew he wanted to be a comic. He started performing on *Saturday Night Live* in 1980, and in 1982 his album of stand-up material was nominated for a Grammy Award. He starred in the remake of the Jerry Lewis film *The Nutty Professor* in 1996. He performed a variety of characters for that movie. He also starred in the Dr. Doolittle movies, and has done voices for Mushu in *Mulan* and the donkey in *Shrek*. This activity will help you create a comedy routine based on impressions.

Try doing impressions of different famous people. Listen closely to how they talk: the tone of their voices, the way they say words, and if they speak fast or slowly. Watch closely the way they move: how they walk and stand, how they use their hands and make gestures, and especially their facial expressions. When you find one you can do well, put that person in an unusual situation. Here are some examples.

- What if Elmo were President? Say some things in Elmo's voice that the President would say.
- What if a Teletubby were a rock-and-roll star? Sing a rock-and-roll song as a Teletubby.
- Listen to a song over and over so that you can re-create the way the singer sings as closely as possible. Then exaggerate it.
- Do impressions of inanimate objects. Imagine what it would be like to be an object such as a rock. Think about how it would talk and say things it might say. What would a popcorn kernel say before it pops? What would a mailbox say about all the letters deposited inside it all day? What would a cheap imitation toy say to a brand-name one?

2

Comic Material

Believe it or not, the best way to get a laugh is not usually to tell a joke. For the most part, the best comedy you can perform is about yourself. You can find humor in things that you know and that mean something to you, and you can communicate that humor to others to make them laugh. The beginning of this chapter has ideas and activities to help you find the comedy in your life and in yourself.

Comic material has been around since the beginning of laughter. In ancient Greece, play festivals were held to honor Dionysus, the god of wine. Playwrights had to write three dramas and one satire or comedy as part of these festivals. Aristophanes wrote some of the earliest comedies known for those festivals.

By the fourth century B.C., comedy surpassed tragedy as the dominant form of entertainment. During the Italian Renaissance, there was a style called *commedia dell'arte*, which included set characters who were exaggerated. The humor came from the exaggerated characters and from the physical acting they would do, called *slapstick*. The charac-

ters fell into specific roles, such as lover, villain, and clown. They got into silly conflicts that often involved chase scenes and hitting one another in silly ways. This chapter will explore slapstick comedy as a source of material and provide a game to experience it called **I Get Knocked Down**.

Another type of comic material involves poking fun at something. There are a few different terms to describe this style. A *parody* is a humorous imitation of something in literature or music. To *spoof* (used as a verb) something means to joke around about it. It can also be a noun referring to a kind of parody, joke, or hoax on someone. A *satire* is

> *The lazzi refers to standard speeches or bits of business done by commedia dell'arte characters.*
>
> *A sitcom is a comedy about funny situations the characters get into. The term sitcom comes from combining part of the words situation and comedy.*

a spoof that pokes fun at something to make it look foolish or ridiculous. The word *satirical* comes from satire. Parodies are further explored in this chapter, along with the game **Movie Trailer Madness.**

William Shakespeare wrote 14 comedies. He often used *puns* or plays on words to communicate his humor. This chapter contains more information on puns and a game called **Love Letter** that is full of them. By the end of this chapter, you'll have a lot of ideas for material to make people laugh.

Check Your Attitude

One or more players

Your attitude is how you feel about the things around you. This is a great area to mine for comic material.

Props

Pen
Paper
Watch with a second hand

List at least three things after each attitude listed below:

Things I love

_____

_____

Things I hate

_____

_____

Things that are stupid

_____

_____

Things I am proud of

_____

_____

_____

Things I am frightened of

_____

_____

_____

Things I am worried about

_____

_____

_____

Choose one topic and attitude from your list and talk out loud about it for at least one minute. If you run out of things to say, just keep repeating the attitude and the topic, such as "I hate my orthodontist, I hate my orthodontist," and so on. You can also try writing about your topic and attitude. Use a chain-of-thought method of writing. Don't let your pen lift off the paper. Just keep writing. See if anything funny emerges from these brainstorms.

Next, try the same exercise with the same topic, but with the opposite attitude. Find a reason for the change in attitude. For example you might say, "I love my orthodontist. I love how she tightens my braces so tight I can't eat brussels sprouts."

Another way to find comedy in your life is to make comparisons. Compare two things in your life and improvise or write about it. To *improvise* means to act without planning in advance what will happen. Here are some examples.

- Compare your pet's life to a human's life.
- Compare a video game to real life.
- Compare a cartoon character to a real person.
- Compare your fashion to your parents' fashion.

Tell others about your comparisons. See what others find most humorous, and if they have ideas to add to yours.

Comedy in Your Friends

One or more players

To find the comedy in things around you, make a list of unusual things in your life. Do you have an unusual hobby, family, or friend? To find some ideas about what could be unusual about a friend, play this game.

A *simile* is a comparison of someone or something to an object and saying what they have in common with that object. For example, you might say your friend is like a circus because she is a lot of fun. One way to develop a character is to think of a simile for him or her. This game is all about similes, but it can get really funny when you start thinking of your friends as the objects, and doing funny things that the objects do.

Sit in a circle and have one player go first by saying a simile about the person on her right. For example, you can say, "My friend Bob is like a muffin because he's warm." Go around the circle and have everyone give a different way that Bob is like a muffin. Don't worry if it's not true, and don't try too hard to make sense. The humor comes when you describe the muffin, and we think about Bob that way.

If you are playing this game by yourself, write down all of the examples you can think of. Here are some examples.

Bob is like a muffin because

- He is homemade.
- He is full of nuts.
- He is low-fat.
- He smells good.

Continue the game until everyone has had a turn to make up similes for each other.

In *Alice in Wonderland,* the Mad Hatter asked Alice a riddle. He says, "Why is a Raven like a Writing Desk?" Alice doesn't know the answer, and the Mad Hatter says he doesn't know either! In the book the riddle never gets answered. The answer is "because Poe wrote on both," meaning that Edgar Allan Poe wrote on a raven (about a raven) and actually wrote on (the surface of) a writing desk.

Comedy in Yourself

Two or more players

To find the comedy in yourself, you must be willing to laugh at yourself. If you have unique characteristics, they can be used in your comedy. To find out if you have a unique physical trait, ask people what they notice first when they look at you. Make a list of the things they say. Play this game to see how others see you, and to see how a little movement you do can become exaggerated and turn into physical comedy. You will also use your observation skills as you try to do exactly what other players do.

Divide into two teams. One team (Team A) stands in front of the other team (Team B). Team A does nothing but stand there. Team B watches Team A closely and observes everything they do. That is, they note their actions including body postures, nervous grins, and so on. After three minutes, the teams switch places. Now Team A sits, while Team B stands in front of them. Team A now watchs Team B, closely observing everything they do. After three minutes, the teams switch places again. Team A (now standing) does exactly what Team B (now sitting) just did. After a minute switch teams.

Continue in this way for a few rounds and see what happens. Often something as little as a scratch becomes bigger and bigger each round until it is so exaggerated that it becomes extremely funny. Another thing you will notice is your posture. If you slouch in this game, the other team will pick up on it and show you how it looks from the audience. (Slouching is a big no-no in theater, especially when you have to project your words so the audience can hear your lines.)

If you observe the Disney animated movie 101 Dalmations *closely, you'll find that the animators snuck in several characters from* Lady and the Tramp. *Animators included these characters as an inside joke. Look in the crowd scenes to see if you can find these duplicate characters.*

Slapstick

The term *slapstick* refers to a boisterous loud comedy, one with exaggerated characters and movements. The term comes from the paddle used in farces and pantomimes to make a loud sound when an actor was hit by it. You could hit the actor very gently so as not to hurt him, but the paddle would make such a loud sound, it would seem to the audience that he was hit rather hard. For whatever reason, someone being hit in a funny way, so the audience knows he is not really hurt, can be funny. Someone falling down can also be very funny (but only if they're not really hurt).

Molière was a French playwright who wrote in the style of farce and slapstick comedy. In his play *A Doctor in Spite of Himself*, there is a scene where the husband chases his wife around, hitting her with the slapstick. She then grabs the slapstick and hits him back. The actors who play these roles have to pretend to be hurt in funny ways, not in seri-ous ways, because a scene about someone hitting someone else is not funny unless it is portrayed more like a cartoon. In Bugs Bunny cartoons, for example, it is funny when Bugs stomps on Elmer Fudd or knocks him down because Elmer Fudd is a cartoon character, and the audience knows he cannot really get hurt.

A knee slapper *is a term used for a joke because when some people laugh, they slap their knees.*

I Get Knocked Down

Two players

This game demonstrates the humor of slapstick comedy. The actor relies on exaggerated characters and being hit on the head for humor.

Props

Something you can hit someone on the head with that will not hurt him, such as a pillow, foam tube, or paper towel cardboard tube

One player is the bopper and the other is the actor. Have them stand next to each other, facing the audience. The bopper bops the actor on the head gently so as not to hurt her. The actor pretends that the bop to the head knocks her out, and she falls to the ground in a funny way. She then gets up, but pretends that the bop to the head turned her into another person. She starts talking like this other person, improvising things that person would say. She continues for a few moments until the bopper bops her on the head again. She falls to the ground again, and then gets back up as a completely new character. Once again, she improvises as that character until she is bopped on the head a third time. She comes up as a third character, improvises for a few moments, and then passes out.

Here's an example of how this game might go. Howie and Kathy are playing. Howie is the bopper and Kathy is the actor.

Howie bops Kathy on the head.
Kathy falls down, and then gets back up as a queen.

Kathy: Oh, hello, my loyal subject. You may rise in the presence of your Queen. Don't you just love my crown? It's pure gold, you know.

Howie bops Kathy on the head.
Kathy falls down and then gets back up as a zombie.

Kathy: I have been dead for 3,000 years. But now I roam the earth in search of brains to eat.

Howie bops Kathy on the head.
Kathy falls down and then gets back up as a cheerleader.

Kathy: Go, team, go! Hooray! What a great play! Yay, team!

Kathy passes out.

Mel Brooks is a filmmaker who satirized different kinds of films, such as monster movies in **Young Frankenstein** and science fiction movies in **Spaceballs**.

Movie Trailer Madness

One or more players

There are many ways to create a parody of something. You can parody a fairy tale by modernizing it, changing the setting or characters, or changing the point of view. Here are some examples.

- The musical *The Wiz* modernized the story and setting of *The Wizard of Oz*.
- You can change the gender of Cinderella. She can be a boy called Cinder Fella.
- The book *The True Story of the Three Little Pigs* is a version of this well-known tale told from the wolf's point of view.

Many television shows use this style of humor, too. *The Simpsons*, for example, spoofed Mary Poppins by calling their nanny Shari Bobbins, and *Sesame Street* has spoofed the Beatles song "Let It Be" by calling it "Letter B."

You can spoof famous movies by playing this game. A *movie trailer* is the preview that you see for a movie when you go to see a different movie. This fill-in-the-blank game involves practicing your grammar as well as your improv comedy skills.

Choose a famous movie. Decide on certain parts of the movie, such as phrases or characters that could be replaced by another word or words. Ask the audience or other partic-ipants to give you those words, without knowing how you will use them. Then narrate a movie trailer using the audience suggestions. For example, if you want to choose a scary movie, you might choose *Dracula*. The basics of the real movie are as follows: Dracula is a vampire who lives on blood, and the only way to stop him is to drive a stake through his heart. Ask the audience to suggest a liquid (such as lemonade), an object (such as a trumpet), and a part of the body (such as a nose). In the story of *Dracula*, replace blood with the new liquid (lemonade), the stake with the new object (the trumpet), and the heart with the new part of the body (the nose). Here's the improv that might result from these suggestions:

> *"Coming soon, to a theater near you . . . Dracula! The most feared creature of all times. He lives by sucking lemonade from unsuspecting lemons. See how he is stopped by a hero who manages to drive a trumpet into his nose! Don't miss Dracula!"*

If you like, have others act out the movie while you narrate it.

Here's how the game might work for *Frankenstein*. The basics for the real movie are as follows: Dr. Frankenstein creates a monster out of dead bodies, but the monster is misunderstood, so the townspeople destroy him. Ask the audience for a man's name (such as Josh), an object (such as a noodle), and an adjective (such as *silly*). (An *adjective* is a word that is used to describe other words.) In the story of Frankenstein, replace Frank with the new name (Josh), dead bodies with the new object (noodles), and misunderstood with the new adjective (silly). Now improvise the movie trailer for the new version of *Frankenstein*:

"Coming this fall, don't miss Joshenstein! Dr. Joshenstein has been working in his laboratory, creating his monster made from fresh noodles! Watch his noodle creation come to life! See how the townspeople react because he is just too silly. He is so silly he must be destroyed. Joshenstein, in theaters soon."

The Wolfman is another famous scary movie that works well with this game. The basics for the real movie are as follows: He's half man and half wolf, and the Wolfman prowls the streets of London. The only way to stop him is with a silver bullet. Ask the audience for an animal (such as a hamster), a town (such as Detroit), and an object (such as a feather). In the story of the Wolfman, replace wolf with the new animal (hamster), London with the new town (Detroit), and bullet with the new object (feather). Here's an improv that might result from this new version of *The Wolfman*:

"You can run, but you can't hide. He's half man, half hamster! That's right, Hamsterman is on the loose! People of Michigan beware because Hamsterman is roaming the streets of Detroit. Watch our heroes as they use their special silver feather to put a stop to Hamsterman. Will the feather tickle him? Find out. Come see Hamsterman in theaters now!"

As an inside joke, the director of the horror film The Howling named the characters in his film after all of the directors of past Wolfman films.

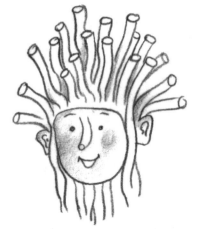

Puns

A *pun* is a humorous use of two words having the same or similar sounds but different meanings. The punch lines of knock-knock jokes are usually puns. Here's an example.

Knock knock!

Who's there?

Olive!

Olive who?

Olive you!

Olive you is a pun or a play on the words "I love you."

Here's another:

Knock knock!

Who's there?

Sam and Janet!

Sam and Janet who?

Sam and Janet evening.

Sam and Janet evening is a pun or play on the song title "Some Enchanted Evening."

Can you really tickle your funny bone? Your funny bone *is the part of your elbow that makes you feel a tingling sensation in your arm and hand when it's hit a certain way. It also refers to a person's sense of humor.*

Love Letter

Any number of players

Here is a game about fruits and vegetables being used as puns. Replace the numbers with the names of fruits or vegetables to create a love letter. Cover the answers on the right-hand side of the page before you begin.

Props

Copy of the following letter for each player

My Dearest Kristie,

First, I want you to know that my heart (1) only for you. (2) you know that we make a great (3)? If you (4) all for me, why not (5) get married. Since we (6), I suppose you will want a fancy wedding. Please, dearest, do not (7) my hopes, because it's love like I have for you that makes a (8) crazy. I trust you will never (9) your nose at me. If you do, the only thing for me to do is go to the river (10) in.

All my love,

Danny

Answers

1. Beets
2. Honeydew
3. Pear
4. Carrot
5. Lettuce
6. Cantaloupe
7. Squash
8. Mango
9. Turnip
10. Endive

Look at the scene from *Rapunzel* (page 139) in Chapter 12 for ideas on how to work puns like this into a scene. You can come up with other letters or scenes based on other kinds of puns. Create a letter using puns about candy, trees, or animals.

3

Making It Funny

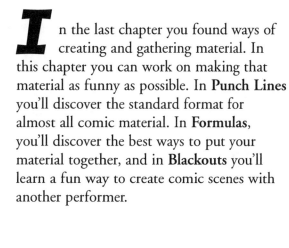

In the last chapter you found ways of creating and gathering material. In this chapter you can work on making that material as funny as possible. In **Punch Lines** you'll discover the standard format for almost all comic material. In **Formulas**, you'll discover the best ways to put your material together, and in **Blackouts** you'll learn a fun way to create comic scenes with another performer.

Punch Lines

There are two parts to a joke or comedy bit: the setup and the punch line. The *setup* is the line or lines that you say that lead to the punch line. There are a number of ways the setup contrasts with the punch line to make it funny. The setup can be usual or normal information, followed by something completely unusual, abnormal, or exaggerated. This is the *punch line*. The punch line is not expected. That's why the audience laughs.

If you have a favorite comic, videotape him performing his routine. See if you can break down his lines into setup and punch lines. Then see what kind of setups were used, and why the punch lines were successful.

Formulas

One or more players

There are some formulas you can use when turning your material from the previous chapter into humor for your routine.

Props

Pen
Paper
Lists from Check Your Attitude game (see page 9)

Look at your lists of things you hate from the **Check Your Attitudes** game. See if you can list at least three reasons why you hate each thing you listed. Put them in order, with the funniest one last. Do the same with the other lists.

You can also do this with the **Comedy in Your Friends** activity (page 11). Look at all the ways Bob was like a muffin. Choose the three funniest, and tell them to someone as a joke. Be sure to save the funniest one for last.

Blackouts

One or more players

For jokes that consist of one line as the setup and one line as a punch line, try performing them as blackout scenes. They are called *black-out scenes* because the lights go out quickly after the punch line is said.

There are a number of ways to create a blackout scene. The first way is to turn a short joke into a blackout scene. If you have three players, choose two to be the actors, and one to control the lights. In theater, that person would be called the lighting crewperson. Begin with the lights off, and have the two actors stand in front of the audience. When the lights come on, one actor asks the other actor the first part of the joke. The other actor says, "I don't know," and repeats the first part of the joke. The first actor then says the punch line. As soon as the punch line is said, the third player controlling the lights quickly turns them off. Here's an example of how this type of blackout scene might go.

It begins with the lights out. Jamal and Wendy are standing in front of the audience. Maya is controlling the lights.

Jamal: Why did the chicken cross the playground?

Wendy: I don't know. Why did the chicken cross the playground?

Jamal: To get to the other slide!

Maya turns out the lights.

If you are performing by yourself, stand near the light switch, say your setup to the audience, pause for a moment, then say your punch line and quickly turn out the lights.

Another way to create a blackout scene is to think of a famous line or sentence. It can be from a movie, history, literature—anything as long as it's well known. Then think of funny second lines to say after the original line is spoken. Here are some examples.

If the line is "Toto, I have a feeling we're not in Kansas anymore," made famous by Dorothy in *The Wizard of Oz*, there are a number of funny things that can be said after it, such as:

- No kidding!
- Maybe we're in Detroit.
- What are you talking to me for? I'm just a dog!
- Woof!

Choose three lines that you think are the funniest. Then perform them, putting the best one last.

Three is a magic number in comedy. Things that are funny often happen three times to get the best results from an audience. If they were to be done four times, the audience might tire of the joke, but three seems to be the right number of times for the audience to enjoy the humor the most. Think of it this way: If you say something that makes the audience laugh once, it's funny. If you immediately follow it with something else that makes the audience laugh, it's funnier. Immediately following that with something that makes them laugh a third time is funniest.

   For this example choose one player to be Dorothy, one to be Toto, and one to run the lights.

The crewperson turns off the lights.
Dorothy and Toto stand in front of the audience.
The crewperson turns the lights on.

Dorothy: I have a feeling we're not in Kansas anymore.

Toto: No kidding!

Crewperson turn the lights off.
(Pause for laughter.)
Crewperson turn the lights on.

Dorothy: I have a feeling we're not in Kansas anymore.

Toto: Maybe we're in Detroit.

Crewperson turn the lights off.
(Pause for laughter.)
Crewperson turns the lights on.

Dorothy: I have a feeling we're not in Kansas anymore.

Toto: What are you talking to me for? I'm just a dog!

Crewperson turns the lights off.
End of scenes.

   Another idea for a series of blackout scenes is to come

up with three different answers to a joke. For example, there's an old joke that begins, "Waiter, there's a fly in my soup." The waiter's response changes with different versions of the joke. Come up with three responses for the waiter, and turn them into three blackout scenes. Here's an example with a light crewperson, a customer, and a waiter.

The crewperson turns the lights on.

Customer: Waiter, there's a fly in my soup.

Waiter: Be quiet or everyone will want one.

The crewperson turns the lights off.
(Pause for laughter.)
The crewperson turns the lights on.

Customer: Waiter, there's a fly in my soup.

Waiter: What's it doing there?

Customer: The backstroke.

The crewperson turns the lights off.
(Pause for laughter.)
The crewperson turns the lights on.

Customer: Waiter, there's a fly in my soup.

Waiter: Don't worry, it doesn't eat much.

End of scenes.

Canned laughter *is fake laughter often used in sitcom television shows. It is called canned laughter because sound effects used to be made in a device that looked like a can. When you opened the can, the sound would come out, similar to a music box.*

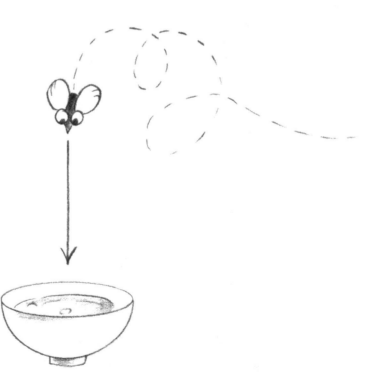

4

Comic Style with Props

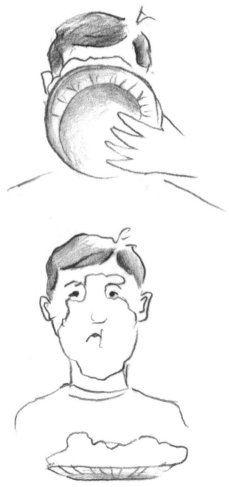

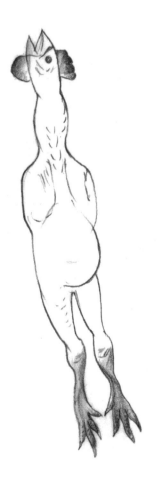

Many comics use objects in their routines. Gallagher is a comic who goes so far as to smash watermelons that squirt all over his audience. A rubber chicken is a famous comic prop, and a pie in someone's face is known for its comic value, too. This chapter will show you how you can use objects in funny ways. You will also find games with fun ways to play with funny objects. Routines in the style of Charlie Chaplin (Chapter 1) can be created with the activity **Trouble with a Small Object**. Everyday objects become the source of comedy in **Use That** and **Anything Puppets**. Puppets and stuffed animals are used in **Safari**, while material and scarves help you become aliens in **Alien Hot Seat**. You can use objects to get to know other people in a group with such games as the *M&M's* **Game** and **Toilet Paper Game**. Finally **Toilet Paper Costumes**, **Funny Faces**, **Photo Captions**, and **Fictionary** are party games that use objects as well as creativity.

Trouble with a Small Object

Two or more players

If a director wants actors to use their body and facial expressions more, one thing she can do is have them pantomime their scenes. *Pantomiming*, or acting without words, forces you to communicate with your body and facial expressions. Because there was no sound in old movies, comic performers like Charlie Chaplin had to be great at pantomime. This is a charades or pantomime game, so you don't use words or your voice, just your face and body.

Think of a small object that you can have trouble with such as a pair of scissors, a can opener, or a doorknob. Act out a scene where you are having trouble with that object. Exaggerate your trouble physically. Let your face show how frustrated you are. Really use your hands and body to show what's wrong with your object. After you have performed for a few minutes, have others guess your object.

Here are some ideas for objects:

- Broken watch
- Jar with the lid on too tight
- Ketchup package you can't get open
- Map you can't fold right

Use That

Two or more players

This game works with two players or two teams of players. Players use their imagination and come up with funny ways to use objects.

Props

2 objects of different shape and size

Divide into two teams. The teams stand on opposite sides of the room. At the same time, each team begins with its object. Someone from the first team must pretend to use the object in a way it is not normally used. For example, if it is a Frisbee, she might wear it as a hat. As soon as you can tell how she is using the object, say "switch!" The other team must immediately use its object in a way it is not normally used. For example, if it is a brush, someone from the team might sing into it like a microphone. Continue switching between teams until one team is out. Once one team is out, the other team is the winner. Here's how you get out.

1. If you repeat a way that has already been used in this round, even if it was used by the other team for the other object, your team is out.
2. If you use your object for something too similar for what it is normally used for, your team is out. For example, using the brush as a comb is too close to what the brush is normally used for.
3. If you pause or say "um . . ." when it is your team's turn, your team is out.

Here are some ideas for objects to use:

- Hula hoop
- Cooking pot
- Broom
- Jump rope
- Traffic cone
- Wig
- Empty wrapping paper tube
- Hat
- Paper plate

More Laughs

Play **Use That** pretending to be aliens who have found earth objects and don't know what they are for.

The Martians on Sesame Street are scared by such earth objects as clocks and telephones. The design of the Martians was inspired by Elizabeth Taylor's headdress in the movie Cleopatra.

Anything Puppets

One or more players

You can work **Anything Puppets** into your comic routine without the use of a puppet theater. See how to give inanimate objects lives of their own with impressions. (See Chapter 1 for more ideas.)

You've probably heard of making puppets out of socks or paper bags. Anything can be a puppet, and using household objects as puppets can lead to very funny puppet shows.

Props

Household objects that you can easily hold in one hand
A puppet theater, which can be made by draping a sheet over a table

Find some household objects and imagine a character for each. Think of what the characters might complain about.

- A fork might complain about being stuck into food all the time.
- A toothbrush might not like being inside people's mouths.
- A can of hairspray might feel like it is spitting sticky stuff all the time.
- A candle might be afraid of burning down.
- A shoe might complain of smelly feet.
- A toilet brush might complain of having to clean toilets.

You can make up funny names for these characters, like Harry the Hairspray, or Jim Shoe.

Create a puppet show where each object gets to tell its story about what it doesn't like. Here are some tips for helping your puppet show emotion even without a face. It's all in the way you move the puppet.

- For happy, move the puppet as if it is jumping up and down with joy.
- For sad, move the puppet slowly, and have it face the floor as if it is drooping.
- For scared, make the puppet jump.
- For mad, make the puppet shake with anger.

More Laughs

If you are playing this game with a large group of people, each person gets one object and writes a monologue about what it would be like to be that object. A *monologue* is a long speech in a play said by one actor to another actor, or to no one, that expresses emotion and/or gives important information to move the play along. Put three to five monologues together to form one puppet show. Puppeteers need to come up with a way to solve their characters' problems.

Safari

Two or more players

In this game, players use props to create animals on a funny safari.

Props

Any animal toys such as masks, puppets, stuffed animals, and so on

One player is the safari leader. The safari leader should think of a character to be throughout the entire scene, and pretend that he is being videotaped on his adventures in the jungle. He introduces the scene. Here's an example:

Safari Leader: Hello and welcome to Safari. Today we're in the treacherous jungle. We never know what kind of animal we'll meet.

One at a time, the other players enter using their props. As they enter, the safari leader improvises about each character based on his or her prop. For example, the first player enters with a kitten puppet.

Safari Leader: Ah, here comes a creature now. It appears to be the rare barking tree kitten.

The player with the puppet makes the puppet bark.

Safari Leader: These creatures are known for barking so loud that bark falls off trees.

The player with the puppet barks even louder.

Safari Leader: Now watch as the barking tree kitten chases after its prey.

The player with the puppet makes the puppet run off stage. The next player enters wearing a bird mask.

Safari Leader: Now it seems we are in luck because here comes the large dododo bird. You may have heard of its relative, the dodo bird. It's time for the dododo bird to lay its eggs. Let's watch.

The player with the bird mask pretends to lay eggs.

Safari Leader: Wasn't that amazing? Now watch the dododo bird fly backward.

The player with the bird mask exits while pretending to fly backward.

This is an improv game, so it's important to remember to play the "yes" game (see Chapter 7). The humor comes when players listen to each other and work together. The safari leader plays the "yes" game by watching what the prop players do, and the prop players play the "yes" game by doing what the safari leader describes.

Note: If there are only two players, one plays the safari leader, and the other player enters three different times with different props.

Alien Hot Seat

One or more players

Sometimes something as simple as a piece of fabric can inspire some funny characters you can use in your comedy routine.

Props

A scarf or large piece of fabric for each player
1 chair

Every player should have a scarf or piece of fabric. Spend some time coming up with different ways to wear the scarf. Try it on your head, over your shoulders, around your waist, covering your feet, and so on. Each player makes up an alien character based on the way he or she wears the scarf, including a name, the name of the alien's home planet, the reason the alien is visiting earth, and how it arrived here. And, for the sake of this game, the alien must speak in a way earthlings can understand. After everyone has created an alien character, one player sits in a chair and the others gather around her. The player in the chair is in the "hot seat" and should *stay in character* while it is her turn. This means she should speak like the alien, saying things the alien would say. There are no wrong answers in this game, so try not to say "I don't know." The other players ask the alien in the hot seat questions, and the alien must answer them in character. Here's an example of how this game might go.

Player: What is your name?

Alien: (wearing a bright yellow scarf around his head) I am Sunstar.

Player: Where are you from?

Alien: I am from the planet Mercury, closest to the sun.

Player: How did you get here?

Alien: I have a transport device in my head. I just think about a place and then I am there.

Player: Why did you come to earth?

Alien: I wanted to see how earthlings enjoy the sun in the summertime.

Continue this game until all players have a turn in the hot seat.

More Laughs

You can use scarves and play hot seat with themes other than aliens, such as:

- Superheroes
- Animals
- Fairy tale characters
- Monsters
- Ghosts

If you are playing by yourself, improvise out loud or write about your alien character, rather than being interviewed.

M&M's Game

Two or more players

This is a great getting-to-know-you game. It's a fun way for a group of people to learn about one another. Working as an ensemble is important in improv comedy (see Chapter 7 for more information).

Props

Pens or pencils
Paper
Small bags of *M&M's* candy

Sit in a circle. Each player will need paper and a pen or pencil. Each player also needs an unopened bag of *M&M's*. First each player writes down his or her favorite color of *M&M's*. Fold these papers and put them in the middle of the circle. Each player then opens up his or her bag of *M&M's* and divides them into piles by color. One player chooses a piece of paper from the middle, opens it up, and reads what color it says. He then has to say one fact about himself for every *M&M's* he has of that color. For example, if the color he chooses from the middle is green, and he had four green *M&M's* in his bag, he might say:

1. My name is Isaac.
2. I live in a house.
3. I have a sister named Anne.
4. I have a really big cat.

After your turn you may eat all your *M&M's*. Continue around the circle clockwise until everyone has a turn.

More Laughs

For a longer version of this game, and to get to know each player even better, make a chart before you start playing that lists the kind of information each color requires you to tell about yourself.

Here's what the chart could say:

Brown: Basic facts (like where you live or what size shoe you wear)

Green: Something you like to do

Yellow: A place you've visited

Blue: A food you like

Red: Something or someone you love

Then everyone says something about himself for every *M&M's* in his bag, following the chart for what kind of information to say.

Toilet Paper Game

Two or more players

Here is a very funny getting-to-know-you game that will have everyone in a comedy ensemble giggling.

Props

A roll of toilet paper

Sit in a circle. Don't tell the other players that this is a getting-to-know-you game. Just say we're going to play a game. Pass the roll of toilet paper around and tell everyone to take as much off the roll as they think they will need. (This is funny because they don't know what they need it for and because toilet paper is not usually used for games.)

After everyone has taken some toilet paper, explain that each player must share one piece of information about himself or herself for each square of toilet paper he or she took. As each player takes a turn, he or she should rip off one square of toilet paper and place it in the middle of the circle.

Toilet humor *is a term for humor that is in very bad taste. It's best not to use it in your comic routine, because not all audiences enjoy it.*

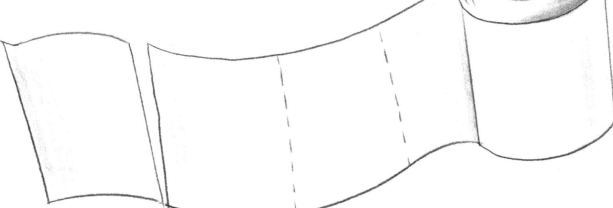

Toilet Paper Costumes

Two or more players

In theater there are many important jobs besides the actors on stage. Designers are artists who create various parts of a play. There are set designers, the people who create the scenery on stage; lighting designers, who decide how to light up the set (in both intensity and color); sound designers, who arrange the music and sound effects for a play; and costume designers, who decide what the actors will wear.

Costumes are not just for Halloween. You can have fun with costumes any time of year, and this activity is an especially funny way to make temporary costumes and see what it might be like to be a costume designer. You might be inspired to create new characters for your comic routine with these toilet paper costumes.

Props

A roll of toilet paper for each group of 2 to 4 players

Players divide into groups of two or more. Each group gets a roll of toilet paper and decides which player will dress up. The rest of the people in the group are the costume designers and dressers. The group of designers creates a costume and dresses up their player using only toilet paper. Designers can wrap toilet paper around the player they are dressing in different ways to create hats, shirts, pants, skirts, dresses, even jewelry! Players can roll the toilet paper and rip it into different shapes and sizes to create their costume.

When all of the groups are done, have a fashion show. Choose one player from each group (not the one dressed in the costume) to be the fashion show announcer. Have him explain the costume while the dressed-up player models it for the other groups. Take turns until all of the costumes have been modeled.

Big Bird's great big costume only weighs about four pounds. Some theme park costume characters actually have fans built into their costumes to cool them down.

More Laughs

You can play this game with a theme. Have the costumes be something specific, such as:

- Medieval costumes
- Designs from different decades, such as the 1950s or 1970s
- Wedding gowns
- Gods and goddesses
- Kings and queens
- Scary creatures

You can choose some players to be judges and have a beauty contest instead of a fashion show.

Funny Faces

One or more players

You can create some very funny faces with this game. If you like, you can even turn these faces into funny characters that you can name and act out in your comic routine.

Props

Pictures of faces from magazines
Scissors
Paper
Glue or tape
Markers or crayons to draw pictures
5 small bowls

Each player cuts out from magazines or draws on separate pieces of paper the following:

- Pair of eyes
- Pair of ears
- Nose
- Mouth
- Hair

Put all the eyes facedown in one bowl, all the ears in another, and so on, so that there is a different bowl for each part of the face. Each player takes a blank piece of paper and draws the shape of a face on it. Then each player chooses one piece of paper from each of the bowls. Glue or tape the parts of the face onto the face you have drawn and see what kind of funny face is created. Give your face a name, too. Take turns so that every player can introduce his or her funny face to the group.

Photo Captions

Any number of players

This is a creative writing game as well as a funny party game. If you are playing this game at a birthday party, use a lot of photos of the birthday girl or boy, from when she or he was a baby all the way through today. If you want to come up with more funny material about your friends (see Chapter 2), use photos of them for this game.

Props
Pictures from magazines or snapshots of people in interesting poses and positions
White paper
Scissors
Glue
Pens

Select pictures to use in this game. Cut out circles from the white paper to be word bubbles like those above characters in comic strips. Glue the word bubbles onto the pictures you have chosen. Place them above the characters so that they become empty word bubbles for those characters. Write what you imagine the pictured person is saying or thinking inside the word bubble. Next, create a photo caption for each of the pictures. A *photo caption* is a sentence or two that describes who is in the picture and what is happening. To think of what to write, look at the poses or positions of the people in the picture and imagine something funny they might say. After all of the word bubbles have been filled in, each player shares his or her pictures and captions with everyone else.

Sesame Street *has characters that are spoofs on famous people, such as Meryl Sheep (instead of actor Meryl Streep) and Placido Flamingo (instead of opera singer Placido Domingo).*

Fictionary

Four or more players

In this game you get points for having knowledge or for being funny, so be creative.

Props

A dictionary
Paper
Pens or pencils

All players sit with paper and a pen or pencil. One player looks through the dictionary to find a word that she thinks the other players don't know. She says the word out loud and spells it. The other players write the word down. Next, the players write a definition of the word. If they know what the word means, they should write the real definition. If they don't know what the word means, they should make up a funny definition for the word. When all players are ready, they take turns reading their definitions out loud. After all players have read their definitions, the real definition is read. Any players who wrote the correct definition get a point. Vote on which incorrect definition is the funniest. The player who wrote the funniest definition also gets a point. Continue the game with a new player finding a word in the dictionary. Take turns until all players have had at least one turn to find the word.

The Heffalump and Woozle are characters made up by A. A. Milne for Winnie the Pooh. They look somewhat like an elephant and a weasel, only with bright and colorful dots and stripes. You can create original animal creatures by combining parts from different animals and giving them funny names.

5

Comic Style with Character

Doing characters is like doing impressions (see Chapter 1) except that instead of imitating a person, you behave as if you actually are that person. Games in the previous chapter, such as **Alien Hot Seat** and **Funny Faces**, as well as games in this chapter and in Improv Comedy (Chapter 7), will give you a lot of ideas for using characters in your comic routines. **Three Through the Door** keeps you on your toes as you create three characters quickly in a row. **Rock Star Names** will give you ideas for original characters, and **Take It Back!** explores characters more deeply in a scene situation. Finally, **Candy Shop** is an idea for a comic scene you can act out with your friends.

Comics and Their Characters

Robin Williams was born in Chicago, Illinois. In college he first studied political science, but switched to drama. He began performing as a comic as well as a mime. Then he landed the role of Mork, an alien from the planet Ork, on the television show *Happy Days*, which led to his own show, *Mork and Mindy*, in 1978. He is known for breaking out into many different characters and improvising in his comic routines. When he did the voice for the genie in Disney's *Aladdin*, the animators worked around his improvisations and made the cartoon change to the different characters he portrayed.

Like Lily Tomlin (see Chapter 1), Whoopi Goldberg has also created one-woman shows based on characters she's created from her imagination. Born in New York, Whoopi Goldberg's real name is Caryn Elaine Johnson, but she thought it was boring and so she changed it. One of her most memorable characters is a little African American girl who wishes she had "long luxurious blond hair." She won a Grammy Award for the recording from that show in 1985. Their careers as comics and character actors have led Lily Tomlin, Robin Williams, and Whoopi Goldberg to successful film careers in comedies and dramas.

Rock Star Names

Any number of players

It's fun to improvise scenes based on funny characters. Sometimes all you need to create a great character is a terrific name. This game will show you a way to make up a character name that's individual to you.

Your rock star name is the name of your first pet and your mom's maiden name. For example, if your first pet was named Fluffy and your mom's maiden name is Nelson, then your rock star name is Fluffy Nelson. Once you have a name for your rock star character, make up a scene about her. Think about what she would wear. For example, maybe Fluffy got her name because she wears fluffy clothes. Think about how a rock star named Fluffy might talk and walk. Also think about what kind of music and instrument she plays. Have someone interview you about what it's like to be a rock star.

For another type of character, find your soap opera name. Your soap opera name is your middle name followed by the street you live on. For example, if your middle name is Justin and you live on Asbury Street, then your soap opera name is Justin Asbury. Make up a character using your name and act out a funny soap opera scene with another character or characters. Because this is a soap opera, make the problems big and your performance overly dramatic. Soap opera characters sometimes act overly sad or tragic. See if you can find the humor in acting that way.

For a third type of character, find your science fiction name. Your science fiction first name is the first two letters of your first name followed by the first two letters of your last name. Your last name is the first three letters of your mother's maiden name and the first three letters of the town where you were born. For example, if your first name is Josh and your last name is Propp, your first name would be Jopr (pronounced "jopper"). And if your mother's maiden name is Miller and you were born in Dayton, Ohio, your last name would be Milday. Your entire science fiction name is Jopr Milday. Make up a scene about Jopr Milday and his space exploration.

Three Through the Door

Two or more players

Playing funny characters is a great way to make people laugh. This game gives you a chance to show off three of your favorite funny characters.

The setting for this game is a store. It can be any kind of store you like and can sell anything in the world. One player is the store clerk and another player is the shopper. The shopper must think up three different characters to portray. First, he enters the store as his first character, improvises a short scene with the clerk, purchases something, and leaves the store. As soon as he is out of the store, he turns back around and reenters as his second character. He improvises another short scene with the clerk, purchases something, and leaves. He then immediately returns as his third character, for his third and final scene.

Here are some ideas for characters:

- Real people, such as the president or Michael Jordan
- Fictional people, such as Snow White or Peter Pan
- Occupations, such as a plumber or a doctor
- Types of people, such as a flirty girl or a troublemaker

Make sure that the audience can tell what kind of character you are within the short scene. Here's an example of how this activity might go.

Tom is the clerk and Skylar is the shopper.

(Skylar enters skipping and talks with a lisp. Her first character is a little girl.)

Skylar: Hello, mithter!

Tom: Hello. May I help you?

Skylar: I've been thaving all my allowanth so I can buy mythelf a new doll.

Tom: Well, how do you like this doll?

Skylar: She's thwell!

Tom: That'll be nine dollars.

Skylar: Thankth! Bye-bye!

(Skylar exits and then reenters pretending to carry a sword. Her second character is Robin Hood.)

Skylar: What ho!

Tom: May I help you?

Skylar: I'm here to steal from the rich and give to the poor.

Tom: Well, I'm not rich, but here's some bread for the poor.

Skylar: Thank you, sir. Would you like to join the merry men?

Tom: No thanks.

Skylar: Well, I've got to go stop that Sheriff of Nottingham!

Tom: Good-bye.

(Skylar exits and then reenters pretending to look through a magnifying glass. Her third character is a detective.)

Tom: May I help you?

Skylar: I am searching for clues.

Tom: Clues?

Skylar: Yes. I am trying to solve the mystery of the disappearing diamond. Have you seen it?

Tom: I'm afraid not.

Skylar: Well, thank you anyway.

(Skylar exits. End of scene.)

You know that the magic number in comedy is three. But if you want to do something more than three times, then do it five or seven times. Odd numbers are funnier than even because the audience is likely to laugh hard every other time.

Take It Back!

Four or more players

In **Three Through the Door** players pretended to purchase something from the store. In this game players return items. What your character decides to return and why can reveal interesting and comedic facts about him or her.

Choose one player to be the store clerk. The store can be any kind of store the characters need it to be. Another player decides on a character to play and enters the store acting as that character. The character has to pretend to return something and must give his reason for returning the item. In improvisation, all items are at your fingertips because everything is pantomimed. *Pantomime* means pretending to have an item you don't actually have, by using your body language and hand movements to show the object. After the character player has finished his return, he leaves the store. The next player then enters as a different character. The game continues until everyone has played a character and returned an item. Here are some ideas for characters to be and items to return.

- Jazz musician returning her trumpet
- Superman returning his cape
- Doctor returning her tongue depressor
- Angel returning his halo
- Snow White returning a poisoned apple
- Old King Cole returning his pipe

Candy Shop

Four or more players

Here's an idea for an improv skit for a large group. The humor comes from playing characters based on candy bars and from a punch line at the end of the scene. If you don't have a large group of players, then you can have players perform more than one character.

Props

Poster board
Markers

Use the poster board and markers to make a large sign that reads "Candy Shop." The lettering should be large enough so that the audience can read it, and the sign should be large enough to be held by two people.

When you begin the skit, ask two audience members to volunteer. Have them come up on stage and hold the sign. They hold the sign throughout the entire skit.

The Skit

One player is the candy shop worker. All other players should make up characters based on the names of candy or candy bars. One at a time, they enter and ask if the worker has the kind of candy their character is based upon. The candy shop worker always says no and the candy characters exit the scene. This continues until all players have played at least one candy bar character. Then all the players re-enter and say, "Well, what do you have?" The candy shop worker points to the two audience volunteers and says, "Just a couple of Nerds."

Since Nerds are a kind of candy, as well as an insult, the audience will think it's funny that two of them stood up there for the entire time, holding a sign, only to be called Nerds in the end.

Ideas for Candy Characters

- Three Musketeers—three people who carry swords and say, "All for one and one for all!"
- Lifesavers—a lifeguard
- Milky Way—a spaced-out character
- Smarties—a very smart character
- Sweet Tarts—a very sweet character
- Whatchamacallit—an absent-minded character
- Swedish Fish—a fish with a Swedish accent

There are two kinds of candy with names that mean "to laugh"— Snickers and Chuckles.

6

Comic Style with Music

There are a number of ways comics use music. You can create song parodies, which is when you make up new lyrics to a song. This works best with well-known songs. Musician Weird Al Yankovic has made a living creating parodies of popular songs. Another way comics use music in their stand-up routines is to actually play an instrument as part of their routine. Comic Judy Tenuta was forced to take accordion lessons as a child. Now she uses the accordion in her routine. Other comics play the piano along with their routine, using the music to emphasize the jokes.

This chapter contains funny songs, ideas for making regular songs funny, and some games that warm up your voice as well as your body. Actors and comics use their voices and bodies while performing, so it's important to warm up both. In **Connect the Songs** and **Sing Down** you'll get a chance to sing favorite songs that you already know. Then you can learn some new funny songs, such as **Waddily Acha, Apples and Bananas**, and **Give a Yell!** You can turn songs you already know into hilarious songs with the games **Next Verse**

Same as the First and **Hands Up, Elbows Bent**. Then you can warm up and dance and sing in funny ways with **My Bonnie, The Penguin Song**, and **Hi, My Name Is Joe**. Finally, you can think of all the jokes you know and work them into a **Joke Dance**.

> The term vaudeville comes from the French voix de ville, which means "street voices." It later came to mean stage entertainment made up of acts presented by entertainers.

Connect the Songs

Any number of players

When actors are in a play together or comics are working on a routine together, and when they work well with one another, they're called a good ensemble. Directors and teachers spend rehearsal time building the ensemble, or helping the actors work well together. Here's an ensemble-building game that lets you have a fun sing-along as well.

All players stand in a semicircle. One player starts. That person stands in the middle of the semicircle and faces the other players. This person starts singing any song she wants. At some point another player tags the first player, replaces her in the middle facing the semicircle, and starts singing a different song. The first player takes the second player's place in the semicircle. The new song should be something that the first player's song reminded the second player of. For example, if the first player sings, "My Country 'Tis of Thee," the second player might be reminded of another American song such as "The Star-Spangled Banner," a song that has the word *country* in it such as "Country Road," or a song about anything else the first song makes the second player recollect. The second player continues to sing until another player tags him out and begins to sing a new song.

Here are some rules for being a good ensemble member in this game:

- Don't leave any one player in the middle singing for too long.
- If you can tell the singer is running out of lyrics to sing, or doesn't know the song well enough to sing it for very long, save the singer by tagging her out quickly.
- It's OK to sing along from the semicircle, especially to help the singer with lyrics or melodies.
- Don't laugh at the singer, or stop the game by asking how the singer was reminded of that song.

If you are playing this game by yourself, begin singing a song. As soon as it reminds you of another song, change, and sing the new song. See how long you can go.

Sing Down

Two or more players

This works well as a rainy-day game for a large group and as a two-person travel game. For ideas about songs to parody for your comic routine, play this game with the topics you came up with from the **Check Your Attitude** activity in Chapter 2.

Props

(Needed for the large group version only)
Paper
Pencils
Watch with a second hand

The Large Group Version

Divide into two equal-sized groups. Each group should have a pencil and paper. Decide who will write. A leader must choose a word that appears in many songs, such as *star*, and be the timekeeper. Within a specified time limit, say two minutes, each group writes down as many songs as they can think of that have the word *star* in the lyrics. When the timekeeper says time is up, the groups must stop writing.

   Next, each group counts how many songs they came up with. The group with the highest number of songs goes first. They sing the first song on their list. If the other group has it, they cross it off their list. Then the second group sings a song from their list. If the first group has it, they cross it off their list. Continue singing until one of the groups is out of songs to sing. The group that still has songs on their list is then declared the winner.

The Two-Person Version

In this version, the first player thinks of a word, such as *dog*, and immediately sings a song that has the word *dog* in it. Then the second player has a minute to think of another song with the word *dog* in it. If the second player can think of one, he sings it. Then it's the first player's turn again to sing another dog song. Continue with the same word until one player cannot think of another song in 60 seconds. Award a point to the winner of that round, and let the loser begin the next round with a new word. Here are some ideas for words:

- Cat
- Horse
- Moon
- Sun
- Baby
- Love
- Blue
- Tree
- Ball

More Laughs

Play **Sing Down** with a topic instead of a word. Here are some ideas for topics:

- Songs about farms
- Lullabies
- Songs about food
- Songs about America
- Songs with boys' names
- Songs with girls' names

Waddily Acha

One or more players

ere is a song that uses nonsense words and movements. (See Chapter 9 to learn more about comics who use nonsense words.)

First you need to know the lyrics.

Waddily Acha

Waddily Acha

Doodily Doo

Doodily Doo

Waddily Acha

Waddily Acha

Doodily Doo

Doodily Doo

It's the simplest game

There isn't much to it

All you have to do is

Doodily Doo it

I like the rest

But the part I like best goes

Doodily Doodily

Doodily Doodily

Doodily Doodily Doo

Beep Beep

Next you need to know the movements.

Pat your knees two times, and clap two times for the first "Waddily Acha."

Zig-zag your hands in front of you four times for the second "Waddily Acha."

Touch your nose with your right hand, then your left shoulder with your right hand for "Doodily."

Touch your nose with your left hand, then your right shoulder with your left hand for "Doo."

Repeat for the second "Doodily Doo."

Repeat these movements for the rest of the song.

Touch one hand to your nose for "Beep Beep."

BEEP
BEEP

Apples and Bananas

One or more players

 E, I, O, and *U* are the vowels in the alphabet. Here's a song that sounds silly when you put different vowels in different places.

First, sing the song straight.

> *I like to eat*
>
> *I like to eat*
>
> *I like to eat*
>
> *Eat apples and bananas*
>
> *(Repeat)*

Then replace all the vowels with the *A* sound.

> *A lake ta ate*
>
> *A lake ta ate*
>
> *A lake ta ate*
>
> *Ate apples and bananas*
>
> *(Repeat)*

Next, replace all the vowels with the *E* sound.

> *E leke te eat*
>
> *E leke te eat*
>
> *E leke te eat*

> *Eat epples end benenes*
>
> *(Repeat)*

Continue with *I, O,* and *U.* The song gets especially funny when you say words like *bonono* and *bununu.*

More Laughs

Take a song you already know and try replacing the vowel sounds with different vowels. See which songs are the funniest with which vowels.

There's an old vaudeville joke that goes like this: How do you get to the Palace? Practice, practice, practice! The Palace was the premiere vaudeville theater located in New York. Performers had to practice their routines a lot and become very good to be asked to perform there.

Give a Yell!

One or more players

When you are performing, it's important to project your voice and speak loudly enough for people sitting in the last row to hear you. Here's a song that is more like a cheer with made-up words in it especially for people who like being loud.

There's no tune to this song, just say it as loudly as you can.

> *Give a yell!*
>
> *Give a yell!*
>
> *Give a supersonic yell!*
>
> *And when we yell we yell real loud*
>
> *And this is what we yell:*
>
> *L and M*
>
> *L and M*
>
> *L and M Diego San Diego*
>
> *Ish me Pish me*
>
> *Better not kish me*
>
> *Hocus pocus dominocus*
>
> *Yay, team!*

More Laughs

Make up your own version of **Give a Yell!** Have everyone make up a different nonsense phrase to yell and put them all together after you say, "And this is what we yell."

Many songs use made-up words, such as "Bippity, Boppity Boo" from Cinderella and "Supercalafragilistic" from Mary Poppins.

Next Verse Same as the First

One or more players

Here's another game for people who enjoy being loud. It's a game where you get to sing your favorite songs. You already know that it's important for performers to *project,* or speak loudly enough for everyone in the audience to hear and understand them. There is a difference between yelling and screaming, however. Screaming means making a piercing sound, and it usually hurts your throat. When an actor yells properly, she takes a deep breath and supports her voice, projecting it far and wide. Try this game without screaming, but with good projection.

Think of a short song that everyone knows. Sing it once through as quietly as you can—almost a whisper. Then say:

> *Next verse*
>
> *Same as the first*
>
> *A little bit louder*
>
> *And a little bit worse*

Then sing it again a little louder. Keep repeating the song with the "next verse" part until everyone is singing it as loudly as they possibly can.

Away Down Yonder

Two or more players

This is an echo song. An *echo song* is a song where a leader sings one line at a time and the others repeat after her. To make this song extra funny, try saying the word *whooping* in a funny way. Say it high-pitched and silly. See if others repeat it the same way you said it. Being a funny leader will help you when you are in front of others trying to be funny as a comic.

Leader: Away down yonder

Others: Away down yonder

Leader: Not so very far off

Others: Not so very far off

Leader: A blue jay died

Others: A blue jay died

Leader: Of a whooping cough

Others: Of a whooping cough

Leader: Well, he whooped so loud

Others: Well, he whooped so loud

Leader: From his whooping cough

Others: From his whooping cough

Leader: That he whooped his head

Others: That he whooped his head

Leader: And his tail right off

Others: And his tail right off

You can also use the previous activity, **Next Verse**, with this echo song.

> *The song "I Won't Grow Up" from the musical* Peter Pan *is an echo song.*

Hands Up, Elbows Bent

One or more players

In **Next Verse**, players sang the same song louder and louder. In this game, you get to sing the same song over and over adding movements. This is a great warm-up activity because it warms up your voice and body at the same time.

Before you begin, choose one player to be the leader. Then choose a song everybody knows. Everyone sings the first three lines of the song. Then everyone yells:

    Ooh ah ooh ah ooh ah yeah! (Repeat)

    Then the leader shouts out a direction. Everyone repeats the direction, and then sings the three lines of the song again, doing the direction. The second time the leader shouts out two directions, the third time three, and so on until the last verse when the leader says, "Sit down." Here's an example of playing this game with the song "Row Row Row Your Boat."

All sing: Row row row your boat
             Gently down the stream
             Merrily merrily merrily merrily
             Ooh ah ooh ah ooh ah yeah!
             Ooh ah ooh ah ooh ah yeah!

Leader: Hands up! (Puts his hands up.)

All: Hands up! (Put their hands up.)

Repeat song and Ooh ahs

Leader: Hands up! (Everyone repeats, putting his or her hands up.)

Leader: Elbows bent! (Everyone repeats, bending his or her elbows.)

Continue with the leader eventually saying the following in order:

Hands up
Elbows bent
Knees bent
Knees together
Chin up
Tongue out
Turn around
Sit down

    When players are singing their song with their hands up, elbows bent, knees bent and then together, chin up, sticking out their tongue, and turning around, it is very funny.

My Bonnie

Two or more players

This game is a good warm-up because it makes you think on your feet and on your chair. It's important for comics to think on their feet because they often improvise (see Chapters 7 and 8) and respond to their live audiences.

Props

A chair for each player

The song goes like this:

> My Bonnie lies over the ocean
>
> My Bonnie lies over the sea
>
> My Bonnie lies over the ocean
>
> Oh, bring back my Bonnie to me.
>
> Bring back, bring back
>
> Bring back my Bonnie to me, to me.
>
> Bring back, bring back
>
> Bring back my Bonnie to me.

The game is played by everyone starting the song while sitting in his or her chair. Anytime a word that starts with the letter B is sung, you must stand if you are sitting or sit if you are standing.

The game goes like this:

> *My Bonnie (stand) lies over the ocean*
>
> *My Bonnie (sit) lies over the sea*
>
> *My Bonnie (stand) lies over the ocean*
>
> *Oh, bring (sit) back (stand) my Bonnie (sit) to me.*
>
> *Bring (stand) back (sit), bring (stand) back (sit)*
>
> *Bring (stand) back (sit) my Bonnie (stand) to me, to me.*
>
> *Bring (sit) back (stand), bring (sit) back (stand)*
>
> *Bring (sit) back (stand) my Bonnie (sit) to me.*

The Penguin Song

One or more players

This is a good dance song. It is also a good warm-up because you use different parts of your body as well as your voice. Comics use their voices in funny ways, such as impressions (Chapter 1). They also use their bodies for physical comedy (Chapter 10), so they warm up their body and voice with activities like this one.

Begin by singing this and doing the motions specified:

Have you ever seen

A penguin come to tea

Take a look at me

A penguin you will see

Penguins attention!

(Players stand at attention.)

Penguins begin!

Right arm!

(Players flap a right arm while singing the song again.)

Then sing this:

Penguins attention!

(Players stand at attention.)

Penguins begin!

Right arm! Left arm!

(Players flap both arms while singing the song a third time.)

Continue adding the following one verse at a time with the specified motions:

Right leg

Left leg

Head

(Players nod their heads.)

Turn around

After the last verse say:

Penguins attention!

Penguins halt!

Baby penguins stand on their parents' feet. The ground is too cold for their feet, so they get close to their parents to keep warm. Try that while singing The Penguin Song!

Hi, My Name Is Joe

One or more players

Here's another warm-up song that twists different parts of your body as you sing it. Just like **The Penguin Song**, comics might use this song to warm up their voices and bodies for their routines. There's no real tune to this song, just speak it in rhythm.

Begin by singing this:

> *Hi, my name is Joe*
>
> *I have a wife and a house and a family*
>
> *And I work in a button factory*
>
> *One day my boss said, "Joe, are you doing anything?"*
>
> *I said, "No."*
>
> *So he said, "Turn this button with your right hand."*

(Players pretend to turn an imaginary button with their right hands while singing the song again. At the end of the song select a player to be the boss. He or she says the following:)

> *Turn this button with your left hand*
>
> *Turn this button with your right elbow*
>
> *Turn this button with your left elbow*
>
> *Turn this button with your right knee*
>
> *Turn this button with your left knee*

> *Turn this button with your head*
>
> *Turn this button with your tongue.*

By the last verse players should be twisting their hands, elbows, knees, head, and tongue.

Fred Astaire danced on the ceiling in a movie called Royal Wedding. They filmed it by creating a revolving room so while he remained dancing, the room rotated, making it look like he was dancing on the wall and then the ceiling. Because the camera rotated with the room, it gave the illusion that Fred Astaire was moving, not the room.

Joke Dance

Any number of players

Here's an energy game that will have you laughing and dancing at the same time!

Props

Fun dance music

Every player thinks of a joke. Collectively decide on the order players will tell their jokes. If a joke requires another person to respond or to ask a question of, decide who that person will be. For this game, short jokes work best. Start the music and everyone dances around. The person going first should dance toward the front. Stop the music. Everyone freezes in a fun pose when the music stops. The first player breaks his or her freeze and tells a joke. Everyone then breaks their freeze and laughs. Then start the music again. Everyone dances around, until the second person is in the front. Then stop the music so the second player can tell a joke. Everyone laughs and the game continues until everyone has told a joke. It is important to laugh, even if you didn't think the joke was funny or you had heard it before. It makes the scene more fun and it makes people feel better if their joke gets laughed at.

If you are performing this game by yourself, you can use blackout scenes (Chapter 3), only instead of turning out the lights after the punch line, start dancing.

Comic relief *is the term for a bit of comedy in an otherwise serious play, movie, or book.*

Improv Comedy

I mprov comedy is believed to derive from commedia dell'arte (see Chapter 2). In improv there are no scripts. The actors draw from funny characters they can play and life experience to make their audience laugh.

The hardest part about doing comedy is that it can be scary. It's frightening to be alone in front of others, performing by yourself or even in a group. Improv is a great self-confidence booster. If you practice your improv skills, you'll be confident and ready for anything. This chapter contains games such as **Yes and Let's . . .**, **Yes and I See**, **Ad Campaign**, and the **Team Question Game**, which help teach some of the basic rules of improv. After learning the rules, the next most important thing in improv is to establish a safe environment. **Table Trust**, **Coat of Arms**, and **IAFAT** are exercises designed to do just that.

Ever laughed so hard it hurts? A stitch is a pain in the back or side that can occur from laughing hard. That's why very funny things are sometimes called a stitch.

Self-Confidence

Improvisational comedy is one of the funniest styles of theater. It's also one of the scariest because the actors play in the world of the unknown. Unlike a scene with a script, an improv scene can go anywhere, so the actors performing in an improv scene have to be ready for anything. If improv actors, or improvisers, don't feel safe in the environment where they are improvising, it will be very difficult for them to be funny. They will be thinking too hard about making fools of themselves and being ridiculed. If you are going to be improvising with friends or in a class-room, start by making a list of ground rules that everyone agrees to follow. Here are some to get you started.

A double take *is a comic way to look surprised. Look at what surprised you once, turn away, and then quickly turn back to it and look even more surprised.*

1. **Be positive.** Saying "yes" is the number one rule of improv because if you say "no" in a scene it stops the scene and makes your scene partner feel bad about the idea he improvised.
2. **No put-downs.** Teasing or making fun of another player will make that player hesitate to try new things, and will keep the scenes from being as funny as they could be.
3. **Trust one another.** Now that everyone has agreed to ground rules, work on developing a trustful atmos-phere for everyone.

Can you think of other ground rules to add to this list?

Yes and Let's . . .

Three or more players

The number one rule of improv is to say "yes," or play the "yes" game by always agreeing with your scene partners and going along with what they say. The funniest scenes happen when actors work together. This game is a great way to practice playing the "yes" game and going along with your fellow actors.

The game begins when one person gives a direction beginning with the word *Let's*, such as "Let's walk." Everyone then begins to walk around the room, until someone says, "Yes, let's walk, and now let's dance ballet." Immediately everyone begins to dance ballet until the next person gives a direction. The round continues until someone is out.

How you get out:

1. You must use the correct phrasing. Each direction must start with "yes," then a repeat of the previous direction, then the word *and*, then the new direction. If you forget to say "yes" or "and," you're out.
2. You must repeat the previous direction exactly as the other person said it. For example, if the previous direction was, "Let's kick our left feet," but you say, "Let's kick our feet," you're out because you forgot to include the word *left*.
3. Since there is no order for who gives the next direction, the players must try to cooperate. No one should say all the directions, but there should

also not be too long a pause between directions. If two people give directions at the same time, they're both out.

Continue the game until there is one person left. That person is the winner.

More Laughs

You don't have to play this game with rules and winners. It can be a warm-up or learning game for everyone if you just keep playing even when people don't get it exactly right.

A guffaw *is a loud burst of laughter.*

Yes and I See

Five or more players

This "yes" game shows how a scene can get funnier when the players work together.

Props

4 chairs

Four chairs are placed in a row facing the nonparticipating players. Four players sit in the chairs. Players must come up with a situation where they are observing something. Here are some examples:

- Movie critics watching a movie
- Chaperones watching teenagers at their prom
- Grandparents on a park bench watching their grandchildren play
- Fans at a baseball game
- Kids at the circus
- A bride and groom at the head table of their wedding reception

Players begin by talking about what they see. They take turns and talk one at a time. Each player builds on what the other players see, no matter what is said. No players can say "no" or change what another player says he sees. Here's an example where Margo, Bryce, and Arie are film critics.

Margo: This film is really bad.

Bryce: Yes. And look, that alien is so fake.

Arie: He looks like he's made of tinker toys and plastic wrap.

Margo: I know! And I don't think they should have made him roller skate.

Bryce: Now he's skating after that girl.

Arie: She's trying to scream, but it sounds more like opera singing.

Margo: It is opera singing, and the alien is beginning to dance.

Bryce: Now she's putting a tutu on the alien.

Arie: Yes, a pink fluffy tutu. This is the strangest movie I've ever seen.

As you can see, in improv, anything can happen. Aliens can wear tutus and dance around on roller skates, all because the players are playing the "yes" game. The scene would not work if one of them said, "No, he's not wearing a tutu, he's green and slimy." And another player said, "No, he's not slimy, he's spiky." The audience would not be able to form an imaginary picture in their heads of what the alien looks like if the actors disagree. But when the actors work together, very funny things happen!

More Laughs

Play **Film Critics**. It's just like **Yes and I See**, played with the example situation, only in this game you take a made-up movie title suggestion from the audience for you to critique.

One of Charlie Chaplin's comedy bits involved making his food dance with his fork.

Ad Campaign

Two or more players

Here's another game for practicing saying "yes" in improv.

Props

A table and chairs (If these are not available, this game can be played sitting around on the floor. Just use your imagination to pretend you're at a meeting.)

Sit around a table as if you are at a business meeting. Everyone pretends they are advertising executives who must come up with a new product to market, and an advertising campaign to sell the product. An advertising campaign is the plan a company thinks up to sell their product, including what their commercials will be like, what the packaging will look like, and what their ads in magazines will look like. As each player gives his ideas, the rest of the players must agree out loud and excitedly, as if it were the best idea they've ever heard. The ideas given must then be built on, just as in the previous **Yes and I See** game, until an entire campaign is created. Here's an example with Erin, Matt, Juana, and Leo.

Erin: We've got to come up with a new product.

Matt: How about a homework machine?

Others: Yes! Great idea!

Juana: Let's call it The Incredible Homeworker.

Others: Yes! Great idea!

Leo: The slogan could be "The Incredible Homeworker does it all for you!"

Others: Yes! Great slogan!

Erin: We could get famous kids to be in the commercials.

Others: Yes! Great idea!

The game should continue until a number of ideas have been stated for the ad campaign.

Team Question Game

Two players or two teams of players

One rule that improvisers try to follow is never to ask questions. There are two reasons you should never ask questions in an improv scene. First, all improvisers should be playing the "yes" game at all times, so you never need to ask a yes or no question because you know the answer will always be yes. Rather than saying, "Do you want to go to the store?" simply move the scene along by saying, "Let's go to the store." The second reason to not ask questions is that it puts undue pressure on your scene partner, which is not a nice thing to do. If you say, "What's that person doing?" you've created a person, but you are making your scene partner come up with what he is doing; that is, he must now do the creative work. Instead, say, "Look at that person riding a unicycle!" Then the other player can build on this using the "yes and" principle. It's difficult to get out of the habit of asking questions, so play this game to get all questions out of your system.

Divide the group into two teams. Each team lines up facing the opposite team. The first person in each line steps forward and faces the other person on the other team. Each player asks a question, alternating turns, until one of them is out.

Here's how you get out:

1. If you make a statement (including "I don't know"), you're out.

2. If you repeat a question that has already been said in that round, you're out.
3. If you say "um," you're out.
4. If you laugh, you're out.

This last rule often inspires players to make the questions as funny as possible in the hopes of making their opponent laugh. The player who gets out goes to the end of his team's line. The other player is the winner of that round, and stays in her position to play against the next player from the opposing team. When one player wins three rounds in a row, then his team gets a point and the next player from his team takes a turn. Continue the game until everyone has had at least one turn.

Note: There are some scene situations where it's OK to ask questions, such as in a scene about a job interview.

The song "Do Your Ears Hang Low" contains all questions, no statements.

Table Trust

Five or more players

Since trust is such an important aspect of improvising a good comedy scene, many directors and teachers spend rehearsal time building trust between actors. This activity is one way to build trust among players. Please have an adult supervise this activity.

Props

A table sturdy enough for one player to stand on

One player stands on the edge of a table with her back to the others. The other players partner up and form two lines in front of the table, facing their partner. They link arms with their partner across from them, forming a sturdy bed for the player on the table to fall into. The players say, "one, two, three, trust us!" and the player on the table falls back into their arms. The falling person should keep her body stiff and straight, close her eyes, and trust that the others will catch her. After everyone has had a chance to fall, talk about how it felt to fall, if you were afraid, and if you thought you would get hurt. Also talk about how it felt to catch each other.

It has been said that dictators fear laughter more than bombs.

Coat of Arms

Any number of players

In improv it is important for the group to get along and support each other. This exercise is a great way for people in a new group to get to know one another. It's a good thing to do before the next exercise, **IAFAT**.

A *coat of arms* is the design on a shield used in the days of knights in armor. Often it would have symbols on it, which would represent the knight to whom it belonged. In this exercise you can make your own coat of arms and let people know what's important to you.

Props

Markers
Construction paper

Draw with a marker a shape or outline for your shield on a piece of construction paper. Make it big, so it takes up most of the paper. Then draw lines in the shield, dividing it into four equal parts.

In one part, draw a symbol or symbols that represent something you are proud of such as a trophy; ball or goalposts to represent that you are proud of your accomplishments in sports; paintbrushes, pencils, or an easel to show that you are proud of your artistic talent; a baby bottle, crib, or toys to represent that you are a good older brother or sister. In the next section, draw a symbol or symbols that represent your hobbies and interests such as a computer or mouse to represent that you enjoy spending time using the

computer, a pair of dice or a spinner to show that you enjoy playing games, musical notes or an instrument to represent that you like listening to or playing music. In the third section, draw a symbol or symbols that represent an event in your life that changed you or meant a lot to you, such as a house or key to represent moving into a new home, a hospital bed or stethoscope to represent having an operation, or a diploma or gown to represent a graduation. In the last section, draw a symbol or symbols that represent how you think others see you, such as a sun to represent warm and happy, a silly face to represent funny, or a magnifying glass to represent mysterious.

After everyone in the group has completed their coat of arms, each player takes a turn explaining to the others what his or her symbols mean and why he or she chose them.

IAFAT (I Am Funny and Talented)

Four or more players

There is a term used to describe self-confidence called IALAC. It stands for I Am Loveable and Capable. An improv actor must feel very confident to act without a script and feel that he can be funny to an audience. This exercise seeks to build an improv actor's comedic self-esteem. Here IAFAT stands for I Am Funny and Talented.

Props

Construction paper
Markers

Each player takes a piece of construction paper. All players sit in a circle. On the paper each player writes her name and the words: I am funny and talented. Once complete, every player passes her paper to the person sitting on her right. Each player then writes something nice on the paper about the player whose paper is in front of him. They may also decorate it if they wish. Once complete, everyone passes their paper to the right again and again writes something nice about the person whose paper they now have.

Continue like this until everyone has written something about everyone. Stop when the papers are back with the original player. Go around the circle and have the person to the left read what each player has written about the person on his or her right.

If this game is played with people who don't know each other very well, spend some time talking to each other before doing this exercise. Each player should share a story about something he is proud of, about a role model in his life, or about an important experience he has been through.

If you can, post the IAFATs in the room. If not, every player should keep his IAFAT and bring it back to the next meeting. Other people can add positive comments to these papers at future rehearsals.

Teasing or making fun of someone makes that person feel untalented and makes it more difficult for him or her to be funny. Teasing someone is like ripping up his or her IAFAT. NO one should rip anyone's IAFAT.

Mark Twain said, "The human race has one really effective weapon, and that is laughter."

Improv Games

Many comics use improv in their routines, and many of them have performed with improv troupes. In this chapter you will find games to practice the improv skills and rules you learned in the previous chapter.

Drew Carey started out as a stand-up comic. He went on to have his own sitcom called *The Drew Carey Show*, and he also hosts the American version of a British improv game show on television called *Whose Line Is It, Anyway?* The games in this chapter are similar in style to the games played by the actors and comics on that show.

Make Me Laugh

Two or more players

This game challenges the focus of one player and the comic abilities of another at the same time. When speed and competition are involved, the craziness really comes out!

Props

A chair
A timer or watch with a second hand

Choose one player to sit in a chair. Choose another player to be the first "comedian" and one to be the timer. The comedian has 30 seconds to make the player in the chair laugh. The timer says, "Go," and begins timing the comedian. The comedian may do anything except touch the player. He can tell a funny story or joke, make funny noises, do a funny dance, or anything else, as long as he doesn't touch her. The only rule for the player sitting in the chair is that she has to watch the comedian the entire time. She can't look away. After 30 seconds the timer says, "Stop." If the player did not laugh, have another comedian try to make her laugh. If all the players have tried and were unable to make her laugh, she is the winner. When a player does make the seated player laugh, that player becomes the next one to sit in the chair.

More Laughs

For a speed round, everyone can line up in front of the person in the chair. Each player in line then gets 10 seconds to do something funny and then get back in line. The next player in line goes immediately, takes 10 seconds, and then runs back in line. See how many comedians it takes to make the player laugh.

Break the Curse

Four or more players

There is a superstition that says it is bad luck to say the word *Macbeth* in a theater. The superstition comes from the fact that the play *Macbeth*, by William Shakespeare, is full of witches, spells, and bad things happening to people. The only time it is OK to say "Macbeth" in a theater is if you are seeing or performing in the play *Macbeth*. Otherwise, if someone says the word, the theater is supposedly cursed. There is a way to break the curse. The person who said the word must do a series of things:

1. Go outside the theater doors.
2. Turn around three times.
3. Spit.
4. Knock on the door.
5. Ask to be let back in.
6. Have someone else say it is OK to come back in.
7. Reenter the theater.

This improv game was created to poke fun of the ways to break the *Macbeth* curse and other curses like it. It is also a memory game because the person breaking the curse has to remember all the steps he is being given.

Choose one player to be the person who must break the curse. Everyone else stands in a line behind him. The first person in line says, "To break the curse, the first thing you must do is _____" and she makes up a silly thing the other player must do to break the curse. After she says what to do, the chosen player does it. Then the next person in line tells him the second thing to do, which he does, then the third person, and so on. After everyone has told him their step for breaking the curse, they all yell, "Break the curse!" and he must try to put them all together in order. If he is successful, the curse is broken and everyone cheers. Here is an example of how to play this game. Francis is the person who must break the curse. He is standing in front of Sophie, Carlo, Rashid, and Mary.

Sophie: To break the curse, you must first kick your feet in the air four times.

(Francis kicks his feet in the air four times.)

Carlo: Next, you must cluck like a chicken.

(Francis clucks like a chicken.)

Rashid: Then you have to do two jumping jacks.

(Francis does two jumping jacks.)

Mary: And then you have to sing "Mary Had a Little Lamb."

(Francis sings, "Mary Had a Little Lamb.")

Sophie, Carlo, Rashid, and Mary: Break the curse!

Francis kicks his feet in the air four times, clucks like a chicken, does two jumping jacks, and then sings "Mary Had a Little Lamb." Everyone cheers! The curse is broken!

It is said in the theater community that audiences laugh more when they're cold. When an audience is warm they are more likely to feel tired and not respond or laugh as much. That's why some television studios with live audiences and theaters turn their thermostats down when performing comedies.

Line!

Three or more players

During rehearsals, when an actor forgets his line, he may say "Line" and someone will read his line to him. The person holding the script and telling actors their lines if they forget them is called the person "on book." This improv game explores what would happen if the entire audience was "on book," but because this is improv, there is no real script. The audience and the actors make it up as they go.

Choose two players to be the actors. Decide on, or get suggestions from the audience [the other player(s)] for the following things:

2 occupations

A place

The two actors begin acting out a scene based on these suggestions. At any time during the scene an actor can put her hand out to the audience, signaling that she needs a line. The audience calls out what she should say. She performs a line suggested by the audience, and the scene continues. The actors can gesture to the audience in the middle of a sentence, and as often as they like. The audience might give them a line that makes sense or one that is silly. The actors try to make it work in the scene, no matter how silly. Here's an example of how to play this game. Joaquin and Rebecca are the actors. The audience has suggested a secretary and a politician for the two occupations, and the place is a fast-food restaurant.

Rebecca: Oh, hi, boss. I just took this extra job at this restaurant on my days off because I (she gestures to the audience)

Audience: Want a new car.

Rebecca: Want a new car.

Joaquin: Really? Well if I am elected, perhaps we could (he gestures to the audience)

Audience: Fly to the moon.

Joaquin: Fly to the moon.

Rebecca: Really? Are you for exploring outer space? I would love to go to (she gestures to the audience)

Audience: Pluto.

Rebecca: Pluto.

Joaquin: Don't you think Pluto is a bit (he gestures to the audience)

Audience: Small?

Joaquin: Small?

Rebecca: I think it's cute. Besides, I have the perfect thing to wear. It's a (she gestures to the audience)

Audience: Pair of moon boots.

Rebecca: Pair of moon boots.

Joaquin: I think you'd better trade those in for a pair of Pluto boots instead.

Pocket Line

Two or more players

In this game, players need to be ready to make silly lines fit into their scene.

Props

Paper

Pens or pencils

Players should be wearing clothing with at least three pockets

Two players are the first actors. They must leave the room while the other players write down six funny quotes or lines of dialogue on six separate small sheets of paper. Fold the paper up so that the actors won't be able to see them, and so they will fit into the actors' pockets. Bring the actors back into the room, and give each of them three of the pieces of paper to put into three different pockets. Next, decide on the kind of scene the actors will improvise by giving them a who, what, and where. *Who* means their relationship each other, such as friends, mother/daughter, or teacher/student. *What* is an action that they do together, such as baking, playing with blocks, or fixing a computer. *Where* is the place the scene occurs, such as kitchen, playground, or classroom.

The two actors begin improvising their scene. When an actor comes to a moment in the scene where she is about to explain something or give advice, she reaches into one of her pockets, pulls out a line of dialogue, and reads it as part of the scene. The scene continues until all six pieces of

paper are used in the scene. Here's an example of how this game is played with Amy and Jacob as the actors.

After Amy and Jacob leave the room, these are the six lines that the other players come up with:

1. To be or not to be?
2. It's really snowing out there.
3. I'd like to visit Mars someday.
4. You scratch my back, I'll scratch yours.
5. Hanna Banana plays the piana.
6. You must have been a beautiful baby.

Amy and Jacob reenter the room and put the pieces of paper in their pockets. They choose for their scene a teacher and a student fixing a computer in a classroom.

Amy: Jacob, are you sure you know what you're doing?

Jacob: Yes, Mrs. Jones, I've fixed a lot of computers before. Let me see . . .

(Jacob pretends to look at a computer while pulling out a paper from his pocket and reading it out loud)

Jacob: To be or not to be broken? That is the question.

Amy: Well, it most certainly is broken.

A non sequitur *is a comment that has nothing to do with what is being discussed. Some comedians use nonsequiturs as catch phrases to say when a joke does not go over very well.*

(Amy pulls out a paper and reads it.)

Amy: It's really snowing out there.

Jacob: That's the computer screen. It looks like snow, doesn't it? Oh, I think I've found the problem.

(Jacob pulls out a paper and reads it)

Jacob: I'd like to visit Mars someday.

Amy: That's great, but could you tell me what the problem is?

(Amy pulls out a paper and reads it)

Amy: You scratch my back, I'll scratch yours.

Jacob: Well, I don't want you to scratch my back, but you could give me a better grade this semester. The problem is . . .

(Jacob pulls out paper and reads it)

Jacob: Anna Banana plays the piana.

Amy: Yes, of course, that explains why the computer won't work. Anna must have mistaken the computer keyboard for her piano. Well, thanks for figuring that out.

(Amy pulls out a paper and reads it)

Amy: You must have been a beautiful baby.

Jacob: Thanks.

End of scene.

Paper, Scissors, Rock

Three or more players

This improv game is named after the hand game where two players put their hands out at the same time, but in different shapes. The shapes of the hands determine the winner. In this game, hand shapes determine what scene will be performed.

Pick two people to be the players. The others will be the audience. Ask the audience to suggest three occupations, such as waiter, dentist, and dancer. The two players face each other and call out one of the occupations at the same time. They continue calling out occupations until they say the same one at the same time. Then, they immediately begin improvising a short scene about that occupation that involves some sort of conflict or argument. After a few lines, they face off again, and call out the other two jobs until they say the same one at the same time. They then act out a short scene about a conflict in that occupation. At the end of that scene, they face off, say the last occupation, and act out the last scene. Here's an example of how this game may go. Margo and Nabil are facing each other.

Margo says, "Dentist," while Nabil says, "Waiter."
Margo says, "Dancer," while Nabil says, "Dentist."
Margo says, "Waiter," while Nabil says, "Waiter."

Nabil: Here's your club sandwich with fries.

Margo: Excuse me, but I need ketchup.

Nabil: Here you are.

Margo: I also need mustard.

Nabil: Coming right up.

Margo: And relish.

Nabil: I'll see what I can do.

Margo: Please hurry.

Nabil: I said, I'll see what I can do!

Margo: Oh, and don't forget the gravy.

Nabil: I quit!

(Margo and Nabil face each other.)
Margo says, "Dentist," while Nabil says, "Dancer."
Margo says, "Dentist," while Nabil says, "Dentist."

Margo: Open wide, this won't hurt a bit.

Nabil: Ouch!

Margo: I haven't touched you yet.

Nabil: Ouch!

Margo: I'm just taking a look.

Nabil: Ouch!

Margo: You'll have to open your mouth!

Nabil: Ouch!

Margo: Open up!

Nabil: Don't touch me!

(Margo and Nabil face each other.)
Margo and Nabil both say "Dancer."

Nabil: I just love being in a kick line.

Margo: Me, too.

Nabil: We kick higher than any of the other dancers.

Margo: Of course, I kick a little higher than you.

Nabil: Oh yeah? Watch this! (Nabil kicks.)

Margo: Watch this! (Margo kicks.)

(Both continue kicking until they fall down.)

   The end.

Lollipop! Cucumber! Pickle!

Three or more players

In theater, just as in games, there are rules that actors follow and keep in mind while they are acting in order to perform the best they can for their audience. This game is a fun way to help actors remember three of the rules.

Rule 1: **Speak loudly**. Actors must project their voices and speak loudly so that everyone in the audience can hear them. Most live theaters do not use microphones for their actors. The audience must depend on the actors to speak loudly enough for them to hear the lines and follow the story of the play. To do this, actors learn to breathe properly—through the diaphragm—and support their voices with their breath.

Rule 2: **Speak clearly**. Even if an actor is very loud, the audience may not understand what he is saying if he does not speak clearly. Actors must pronounce their words very clearly, making sure that the audience hears all vowel and consonant sounds. Actors learn not to mumble or "swallow their lines." *Swallowing your lines* means starting a line off clearly, but trailing off with your voice by the end of it.

Rule 3: **Remember your posture**. Except for specific character choices, actors must be careful not to slouch on stage. They stand or sit up straight, and "plant their feet." Planting your feet means making sure you stay solid on the ground (like tree roots planted in the dirt), not swaying and moving around.

Choose two people to act out a scene. If you are working on a play, you can play this game with a scene from the play. If not, give the players a who, what, and where to improvise a scene. As the actors are acting out their scene, the audience serves as the "acting police." They are watching to make sure the actors don't break any of the rules. If they do, the audience lets them know by calling out a word. "Lollipop" means "louder." If the audience calls "lollipop," the actors have to speak louder. "Cucumber" means "clearer." If the audience calls out "cucumber," the actors have to speak more clearly. "Pickle" means "posture." If the audience calls out "pickle," the actors must fix their posture. You can make up other words to remind the actors of other rules. For example, "foxy" could mean "face the audience." It helps you to remember what words to say if they start with the same letter of the alphabet as the words they mean.

To be in a pickle *means to be in an embarrassing situation.*

That-Makes-Me-Laugh Symphony

Up to 11 players

If something is funny to you, it's a good bet it's funny to other people, too. In this game you get to improvise about what makes you laugh. You might even discover more comic material for your routine (see Chapter 2).

Choose one player to be the conductor. The other players stand or kneel facing the conductor, so that the conductor can clearly see everyone. Each player says something that makes him laugh. This will be that player's subject for his part in the symphony. The conductor conducts the players in a symphony by pointing at the person she wants to speak, and then cutting each player off with a gesture when he should stop speaking. When the conductor points to a player, the player tells about what makes him laugh. The player can tell a story or describe whatever it is. If he cannot think of what to say, he should repeat, "ha ha ha," over and over again until he thinks of what to say, or the conductor cuts him off. The conductor can have everyone speak at once or just one person at a time. The conductor can indicate through gestures that the players should get louder or softer. After a minute or so, the conductor gestures that it is time to bring the symphony to an end. The players take a bow.

Here are some suggestions for subjects that might make you laugh:

- Clowns
- Cartoons or specific cartoon characters
- Silly dances
- Silly songs or a specific song
- Jokes or a specific joke
- Comic books or a specific comic book character
- Parties
- Games or a specific game

You can play this game by yourself by choosing a topic and ranting on about it. See how long you can go. This may give you ideas for comic material.

More Laughs

If you are playing this game in front of an audience, take suggestions from them for what makes them laugh.

Emmet Kelly was a clown known for having a sad face.

Beginning, Middle, End

Any number of players

This improv game results in an original fairy tale that you create. It shows the basic outline of a story and the importance of a beginning, middle, and end. Just like a joke, every story must have all three elements to tickle everyone's fancy.

Divide into three groups. Each group decides on a different classic fairy tale or story. One group acts out the beginning of their story, one group acts out the middle of their story, and the last group acts out the end of their story. After a few rehearsals, each group performs their piece for the other groups. Then, see if you can create one story, using these pieces of different fairy tales. You may have to change the scenes around to make it work, and use different characters in different stories. There's no wrong way to do this because you are creating an all-new, original tale. Here's an example where group one chooses *Little Red Riding Hood*, group two chooses *Jack and the Beanstalk*, and group three selects *Cinderella*.

Group one acts out the beginning of *Little Red Riding Hood*:

One day a little girl went skipping through the forest with a basket of goodies for her grandmother. She met a wolf that asked her where she was going. She told him, and he ran ahead of her, while she picked flowers.

Group two acts out the middle of *Jack and the Beanstalk*:

Jack climbed up the beanstalk, where he saw a giant. The giant said, "Fee, Fi, Fo, Fum!" Jack stole a goose that laid golden eggs from the giant, and climbed back down the beanstalk.

Group three acts out the end of *Cinderella*:

The prince tried the slipper on Cinderella. It fit. They were married and lived happily ever after.

Now, everyone comes together to create one story with all three parts. Here's how it might go:

One day a little girl went skipping through the forest with a basket of goodies for her grandmother. She met a wolf that asked her where she was going. She told him and he ran ahead of her. While she was picking flowers she came across a beanstalk. She climbed up the beanstalk, where she saw a giant. The giant said, "Fee, Fi, Fo, Fum!" Little Red Riding Hood stole a goose that laid golden eggs from the giant, and climbed back down the beanstalk. When she arrived at her grandmother's house, the wolf tried a slipper on her. It fit. They were married and lived happily ever after.

More Laughs

Play **Beginning, Middle, End** as a creative writing game. Have three different people each choose a different story and give them each three index cards. Each person should write a short beginning to her story on one card, the middle on another, and the end on the third. Mix and match the cards to create three different stories with different beginnings, middles, and ends. Write a new story based on the index cards.

You can create original tales by yourself by putting together the beginnings, middles, and ends of different stories.

Author Styles

Any number of players

When you think about different authors, think about their style of writing. For example, Dr. Seuss wrote short sentences that rhyme, with funny made-up words and characters. Shakespeare wrote in Old-fashioned English, with words like *thou* (meaning you) and *whither* (meaning where).

Choose three authors that you know and discuss their styles. Then choose two people to improvise a scene. Have them decide on or take suggestions for characters to play and a place to be. After they begin the scene, have a third player call out the first author. The actors continue the scene in the style of the author that was called. After a few lines, the third player calls out the second author, and without stopping the scene, the players continue in the new style. After a few more lines, the third author is called out, and the actors bring the scene to an end in the third style.

Here are some authors who have very different writing styles that you may enjoy:

- L. Frank Baum (*The Wizard of Oz*)
- Judy Blume (real-life coming-of-age stories, such as *Are You There God? It's Me, Margaret* and *Tales of a Fourth Grade Nothing*)
- Eric Carle (small nature characters such as caterpillars and crickets)
- Stephen King (horror)
- Lewis Carroll (*Alice in Wonderland*)
- A. A. Milne (*Winnie the Pooh*)
- Maurice Sendak (*Where the Wild Things Are*)
- J. R. R. Tolkien (*The Hobbit* and *The Lord of the Rings* trilogy)

Here's an example of this game using different authors' styles.

Nicole and Mark are the actors. Their characters are a daughter and father, and they are at a baseball game. Sabrina is calling out the authors.

Nicole: This is a great game. Thanks for taking me here, Dad.

Sabrina: Dr. Seuss!

Mark: Do you like it in these seats? Would you like it with some beets?

Nicole: I do not like beets, Dad I Am!

Mark: Would you like a nice hot dog? Would you eat it with a frog?

Sabrina: Shakespeare!

Nicole: Wouldst thou give me a hot dog?

Mark: To eat or not to eat? That is the question.

Nicole: (calling) Oh, hot dog sire! Come hither!

Sabrina: Lewis Carroll!

Mark: Forget the hot dog, it's time for tea!

Nicole: Things here are getting curiouser and curiouser.

Mark: I say we leave this baseball game and go play croquet.

Nicole: Are you mad?

Mark: Off with your head!

End of scene.

To play this game by yourself, improvise a monologue of a character of your choice. Try doing it in different styles.

Lewis Carroll created the character of the Mad Hatter in Alice in Wonderland because chemicals that were used to make hats were known to cause hat makers to go crazy.

What Should They Do?

Three or more players

Here is a game where the audience or other players get to determine the outcome and the the choices the characters make. See "More Laughs" to play this game as a conflict resolution game, providing skills for solving problems in positive ways.

Two players are the actors, and each must select a character to play and a place to be. They begin improvising their scene. When a character must make a decision, a third player yells "Freeze!" The actors freeze and the third player asks, "What should they do?" The audience or other players then suggest what they think should happen next in the scene. They call it out and then the third player yells "Go!" The actors continue, acting out the audience suggestion, until they come to another decision to make. The third player calls out "Freeze!" again and asks, "What should they do?" and another suggestion is given. The scene continues with this new suggestion and goes for a third freeze and suggestion. After three suggestions, the scene is brought to an end.

Here's an example of how this game is played. Gisele and Joe are the actors. Charlie is the third player. Gisele and Joe's characters are two friends at an amusement park.

Gisele: This is a really fun place.

Joe: Yeah. What should we ride next?

Charlie: Freeze! What should they do?

The audience makes a suggestion, such as "Ride the roller coaster!"

Charlie: Go!

Gisele: Let's ride the roller coaster.

Joe: Wow, there's no line! Let's get on!

Gisele: (pretending to sit in the roller coaster car) I'm scared. I don't think I want to do this.

Joe: I know what will help.

Charlie: Freeze! What should they do?

The audience makes a suggestion, such as "Hold hands!"

Joe: Let's hold hands.

Gisele: OK.

(They hold hands.)

Joe: Here we go!

(Gisele and Joe pretend to ride the roller coaster until . . .)

Gisele: It stopped!

Joe: We're stuck!

Charlie: Freeze! What should they do?

The audience makes a suggestion, such as "Fly down!"

Charlie: Go!

Gisele: Good thing I brought my broom. You brought yours, right?

Joe: I've got it right here. Shall we?

Gisele: Let's go!

(Joe and Gisele pretend to fly on their broomsticks from the roller coaster to the ground for a safe landing.)

Joe: There are some good things about being witches.

Gisele: There sure are!

End of scene.

As you can see from the example, the suggestions may be normal, such as holding hands, or they may be crazy, such as flying. The actors' job is to do their best to make the suggestion work into the scene, no matter how crazy.

More Laughs

Play **What Should They Do?** as a conflict resolution game to learn about problem-solving techniques. Give the actors a problem or conflict to act out. Some ideas for conflict scenes are:

- Two kids: One has a ball and won't share it.
- Two kids: One called the other a name that hurt his feelings.
- Three kids: Two kids are playing together and a third wants to play, too.
- Brother and sister: One wants to play Monopoly and the other wants to play Yahtzee.
- Two sisters: One has to do homework, the other wants to play.

The actors begin improvising the scene. When the conflict arises and an argument begins, another player yells, "Freeze! What should they do?" The audience then gives suggestions for a way to solve the problem. The player says "Go" and the actors continue the scene with the audience suggestion. If the problem is not solved by the suggestion in a few lines, the player says "Freeze," and then says "Rewind." The actors go back to where they were when the conflict first began. Then the player says, "What should they do?" and takes another suggestion from the audience. Continue with suggestions until the problem is solved in a way that makes both characters happy.

Old Mother Hubbard

Two players

In this game you act out what the other player says, then decide what he or she must act out, all the while rhyming! It's a challenge with hilarious results.

Two players stand and face each other. Decide who will be Old Mother Hubbard and who will be the dog. Begin the scene like the nursery rhyme:

Dog: Old Mother Hubbard went to the cupboard to get her poor dog a bone.

After the dog says this, the player portraying Old Mother Hubbard acts it out for four seconds. She pretends to go to her cupboard and look for a bone. Then she says:

Old Mother Hubbard: But when she got there the cupboard was bare, and so her poor dog had none.

The dog then acts disappointed and hungry. Next, the dog makes up a line about what Old Mother Hubbard did next. Such as:

Dog: She went to the store to buy him some meat.

Old Mother Hubbard acts like she is going to the store and purchasing some meat. Then she makes up a line about what happened when she got back. This line must rhyme with what the dog said, such as:

Old Mother Hubbard: But when she got back he was washing his feet.

Dog acts out washing his feet.

Dog: She went to the firehouse to get him a hose.

Old Mother Hubbard acts out going to the firehouse and getting a hose.

Old Mother Hubbard: But when she got back he was tying some bows.

Dog acts out tying bows in his hair.

Dog: She went to the farm to get him some eggs.

Old Mother Hubbard acts out getting eggs at the farm.

Old Mother Hubbard: But when she got back he was shaving his legs.

Continue the game for a few minutes or until players cannot think of rhyming responses. (Note for actor playing the dog: Remember that you want the scene to work well, and you know that the other player will have to rhyme what you say, so be nice. End your sentences with words that are easy to rhyme, rather than words like *orange*, *lasagna*, or *Chicago*.)

An anecdote *is a short account of an interesting or humorous story.*

Mother Goose's Back

Large group of players

ere is a game to play if you are hosting a party or leading a class, and you have time to prepare in advance. This game could be used as a party game or a game to play with a large group of players who don't know each other very well. Players are encouraged to talk to different people in the group, and then act with them in funny scenes.

Props

Markers
Labels

To prepare for this game, the host should write the names of different characters from nursery rhymes on labels. Make sure that there are characters that go together in the same nursery rhymes, such as: Little Miss Muffet and Spider, Jack and Jill, Mary and Mary's Lamb, Old Mother Hubbard and Old Mother Hubbard's Dog. The host or leader shouldn't let the other players see the labels. When you are ready to start the game, put a label on each player's back. This label says which nursery rhyme character he or she will be. After everyone has a label on his back, each player can begin trying to find out who he is. To do this, he goes up to other players and ask one yes or no question. Here are some examples of questions to ask:

Am I an animal?

Am I a boy?

Am I old?

Am I big?

Each player can ask only one question to each of the other players, so the player must talk to a lot of different players to get information about his character. After a player has figured out who his character is, he must then find the other player or players in his nursery rhyme. After all players have figured out who their characters are and found their partner or partners, each should take a few minutes to make up a funny version of his or her nursery rhyme. Then each group performs their nursery rhyme in front of the other groups.

More Laughs

Play this game with fairy tales instead of nursery rhymes. Here are some ideas for fairy tale characters to write on the labels: Goldilocks, Papa Bear, Mama Bear, and Baby Bear; Little Red Riding Hood, Granny, Hunter, and Wolf; Rapunzel, Witch, and Prince. After all players have guessed who they are and found the others in their fairy tale, each group makes up their own short, funny version of their tale and performs it for the other groups.

Burlesque *is a form of comic art characterized by ridiculous exaggeration. One example of a burlesque performer is Fanny Brice, who exaggerated her plainness and awkwardness, turning them into comic traits of a character she created called "Baby Snooks."*

That's Good/
That's Bad

Two players

Sometimes whether something is good or bad depends on how you look at it. In this game you have to look at everything from the opposite point of view, turning good situations into bad ones and bad situations into good ones. Playing the opposites, or looking at things from another point of view, is a great way to come up with comic material (see Chapter 2).

The first player begins by saying something that is bad. If you are playing in front of an audience, take a suggestion from the audience for something that is bad. The second player then says, "That's bad." The first player responds with, "No, that's good because . . ." and makes up a reason why the bad thing could actually be a good thing. The second player says, "That's good." The first player then says, "No, that's bad because . . ." and makes up a reason about how the good thing is actually bad. Here's an example of how the game works.

Robbie: My toy truck broke.

Barbara: That's bad.

Robbie: No, that's good because I got a new one.

Barbara: That's good.

Robbie: No, that's bad because the new one is really slow.

Barbara: That's bad.

Robbie: No, that's good because my turtle likes to ride it.

Barbara: That's good.

Robbie: No, that's bad because it makes my iguana jealous.

Here are some ideas for things that are bad to start the scene:

- My balloon flew away.
- I have a cold.
- I'm afraid of the dark.
- I lost my mittens.
- I have to clean my room.

It takes fewer muscles in your face to smile than it does to frown.

Playing the Opposites

Two or more players

In **That's Bad/That's Good**, the humor comes from playing the opposites. The audience is surprised when a bad thing is good or a good thing is bad, and they laugh. When characters act in the opposite way from what the audience expects, it can be very funny. This game lets you explore the humor of playing the opposites.

Decide on a story to act out, and then choose one adjective that describes each character. Improvise the story, but instead of acting like the word you chose, act the opposite. For example, here's how the adjectives and opposites might work for *The Three Little Pigs*:

- If the wolf's adjective is hungry, play him as full.
- If the first little pig's adjective is dumb, play him as smart.
- If the second little pig's adjective is absent-minded, play him as studious.
- If the third little pig's adjective is smart, play him as dumb.

Now act out a new version of *The Three Little Pigs*.

Three little pigs set out to build houses of their own. The first little pig knew that the wolf in their neighborhood was always full, so he didn't spend a lot of time or money building a house, he just threw some nice hay together and had a comfortable home. The second pig

studied the best way to build a house, and decided that sticks would make a nice log cabin look for his home. The third little pig was not very smart. He spent a lot of money and took months and months to build a house of bricks.

A wolf that was very full and could not eat another thing decided to pay the first pig a friendly visit. When he got there he accidentally sneezed and the straw house blew down. The first pig said, "That's amazing! Can you show my brother how you did that?" "Sure," said the wolf. They went to the second pig's house, where the wolf blew down his house so he could study how the sticks blew in the wind. Then they went to the third pig's house to show him the great trick the wolf could do, but his house was so heavy the wolf could not blow it down. They were very disappointed.

Here are some other ideas for playing the opposites:

- Play Cinderella as mean and the Stepmother and Stepsisters as nice.
- Play the characters from *Winnie the Pooh* as their opposites, with Pooh full, Piglet brave, Eeyore happy, Tigger tired, and Owl dumb.
- Play the Seven Dwarfs as their opposites with Doc dumb, Grumpy sweet, Dopey loud, Bashful outgoing, Happpy sad, Sneezy coughy, and Sleepy wide awake.

More Laughs

Play an improv scene as characters that are opposite from what people normally think they are. Here are some ideas for opposite characters.

- A fast turtle
- A loud librarian
- A fish that hates water
- A dumb professor
- A sweet monster
- A clumsy dancer
- A friendly pirate

More Laughs

If you are working on a play, try acting out your scenes playing the opposite of what your character is really like. Playing the opposites helps actors discover things about their characters that they might not realize. For example, playing the wolf as full might make the actor think about other reasons the wolf might have had for blowing down houses.

An oxymoron is a figure of speech in which opposite terms come together to create a phrase, such as "jumbo shrimp" or "heavy lightness."

Sound Silly

Andy Kaufman was born in New York in 1949. He used to create pretend television shows in his bedroom, and began entertaining at children's birthday parties when he was eight years old. He became a stand-up comic and later landed a role on the television show *Taxi*. The character he played, Latka Gravas, was a foreigner from a made-up country. Because the country was pretend, Kaufman had to make up the language he spoke as well. He used his talent for improv and speaking gibberish to create his own language for the character.

Have you ever heard people talk to a baby? They use nonsense words and sounds called baby talk. The reason people do this is because it makes the baby laugh. Even at such a young age, babies recognize humor and things that are funny. This chapter contains games that use nonsense words and sounds that are humorous to people of all ages. In games like **Ha**, **Boppity Boppity Bop**, and **Zumie Zumie**, players say silly things that might make other players laugh. It's important for comics to overcome their embarrassment about being on stage in front of people. Playing games that make you say silly things is one way to do just that. Then there are energy games, such as **Energy** **Pass**, **Whoosh**, and **Whoosh, Boing, Groovilicious** where sounds become energy that travels from player to player. If you've ever tried to communicate with someone who just didn't understand you, you'll enjoy playing **Ah So Co**, **Ork Ork**, and **Buy My Gibberish**. In those games players try to communicate even though they are speaking nonsense.

93

Ha

Four or more players

This game is popular at slumber parties, but it has a purpose. Drama teachers often use this game to teach proper breath support to their students. When you breathe properly, your diaphragm, located just above your stomach, will move in and out. First, find out if you are breathing properly with this exercise: Put your hands above your stomach with your fingertips touching. Take a deep breath. If your shoulders move up and down, you are not breathing properly. If your fingertips spread apart, you are breathing properly.

Next, try saying "Ha" over and over. See if your diaphragm moves with every "Ha." Another good way to view the way your diaphragm works when you breathe is to lie down on your back with your feet on the floor and your knees bent. Take a deep breath and watch the area just above your stomach rise. That's how actors should breathe when they want to project their voices on stage. You can play the "Ha" game for a fun way to practice good breath support.

One player lies on the ground. The next player lies down with his head on the first player's stomach. The third player lies down with her head on the second player's stomach, and so on, until all players are lying down on someone's stomach. The first player begins by saying the title of the game one time: "Ha!" The second player says it twice: "Ha ha!" The third player says it three times, and so on. Saying "Ha" over and over makes your stomach move up and down, causing the next player's head to move up and down. Continue the game for as long as you can. It usually ends with all players cracking up and laughing.

You can see this game being played on a rerun of **The Brady Bunch.** *It's part of the slumber party episode.*

Boppity Boppity Bop

Six or more players

Using your body in funny ways is a great way to add humor to any comic routine. Here's a game that keeps you on your toes and puts the players in all kinds of fun poses.

Stand in a circle and choose one player to be the "bopper." The bopper stands in the middle of the circle. Here are the general rules.

1. If the bopper goes up to you and says "Boppity, boppity, bop," you must say, "Bop" before he or she finishes saying those words.
2. If the bopper goes up to you and just says, "Bop," you can't say anything at all.
3. When the bopper says, "Attention!" everyone stands at attention, saluting with his or her right hand.

When a rule is broken, the person who broke it becomes the new bopper.

After you have played with the general rules for a while, try adding on. Here are some ideas for add-on rules.

1. Butterfly: If the bopper comes up to you and says "Butterfly," you must put your fingers on your forehead like antennae, and the people on either side of you must become your wings.

2. Elephant: If the bopper comes up to you and says "Elephant," you must make a trunk with your arms, and the people on either side of you must become your ears.
3. Rock Star: If the bopper comes up to you and says "Rock star," you must pretend to play guitar, while the people on either side of you become pulsing speakers.
4. Movie Star: If the bopper comes up to you and says "Movie star," you must pose with your hands under your chin and smile, while the people on either side of you pretend to take your picture.

> **Scat** *is a style of singing in jazz music where the vocalist uses made-up sounds to improvise with the music.*

5. Frog: If the bopper goes up to you and says "Frog," you must squat down like a frog, and the people on either side of you must put their hands into the shape of a circle, to become the frog's eyes.
6. Jell-O: If the bopper comes up to you and says "Jell-O," you must wiggle, and the people on either side of you must put their arms around you like a bowl.

More Laughs

Make up add-ons of your own. Think of animals or occupations and what the pose would have to be if the bopper says the words. For a challenge, have the bopper count to three after he says an add-on, for example: "Frog, one, two, three!" If a player is not in his or her pose in three seconds, that player is the new bopper.

Zumie Zumie

Six or more players

Comics and actors need to stay focused on their routines and scenes in order to remember what to say and stay true to their characters. This fast-paced game will have you laughing all they way up to the very silly end. It's also a great focus game.

Sit in a circle and choose one player to be Zumie Zumie. Then count off with the player to Zumie Zumie's left as number one. The round begins with everyone reciting the following chant:

> *Zumie Zumay (beat)*
>
> *Zumie Zumay (beat)*
>
> *Zumie Zumie Zumie Zumie*
>
> *Zumie Zumay (beat)*

While reciting the chant, and throughout the game, players continuously pat their knees twice and clap twice, over and over, to keep the rhythm. Immediately following the chant, and keeping in rhythm, Zumie Zumie says

"Zumie Zumie," and then a number twice, such as "five, five." The person who is number five says his number twice, and then another player's number twice or Zumie Zumie. The game continues until a player is out.

Here's how you get out:

- If you pause or speak out of rhythm
- If you speak out of order (for example, if you don't say your own number first)
- If you say the number of someone who is out

When you are out, scoot out of the circle a bit, but stay with the game. That makes it difficult for the other players to keep track of who is out, and which numbers they can still call. When someone is out, begin the new round with the chant. Zumie Zumie always starts unless he is out. Then the person with the lowest number starts. When there are only two people left, instead of saying their numbers, one of them is "soup soup," and the other is "soap soap."

> **The term shtick *is used to mean someone's particular running gag or comic routine.***

Energy Pass

Six or more players

Low on energy? No one wants to see a tired comic. If you have energy, so will your audience. This game will perk everyone up!

Players stand in a circle and choose who will go first. The first player turns to the person on her left and makes a quick sound and gesture. For example, she may yell "Ta-da!" for her sound, and jump with her hands up high for her gesture. The player to her left quickly passes that same sound and gesture to the next person in the circle, who passes it on until everyone has passed that same sound and gesture. When it gets all the way around the circle to the person who started it, she says it one more time. Then the person to the left of the first person does his own sound and gesture. For example, he may shout "Hey!" and kick his feet. The person to his left passes that gesture on and it goes around the circle as well. The game continues until everyone in the circle has had a turn to pass along his or her own sound and gesture. This game goes very quickly, with no pausing between passings or before a new person's turn to create a new sound and gesture. The sound and gestures should be big, loud, and energetic!

Whoosh

Six or more players

This game is like **Energy Pass** and will get your energy flowing as well, but it involves a challenge and a race. If you are making up comic scenes or routines with a large group of people, start each rehearsal with this game. Try to beat your time each day. This will give all of you a common goal to work toward, while boosting your energy for the day's rehearsal.

Props

A watch with a second hand or a timer

Players stand in a circle. Choose one player to go first. She pretends she has a giant ball in her hands. As she hands it off to the person on her left, she says "Whoosh!" That person passes the imaginary ball to his left, saying "Whoosh!" and so on until it comes back to the first person. After you have practiced passing the giant whoosh ball around, have someone time you. See how long it takes for the whoosh to go all the way around the circle. Make it your goal to beat your best time whenever you can.

More Laughs

If you have a very large group, divide in half and have whoosh races. Make two circles and see which one can pass the giant whoosh ball around the fastest.

> **A wisecrack** *is a smart, obnoxious remark that can sometimes be funny. If someone is called a "wise guy" it's because he makes wisecracks.*

Whoosh, Boing, Groovilicious

Six or more players

Here's another energy game that involves a silly dance and even a chance to freak out! Try not to be embarrassed or self-conscious when dancing silly or freaking out. These feelings can kill any comedy routine. Play this game to overcome those feelings.

Just like **Whoosh**, this game begins in a circle, and one player starts by passing a giant imaginary whoosh ball to his left. But this time, when the ball comes to you, you have options:

1. Whoosh: You can pass the ball on to the next person in the circle and say "Whoosh."
2. Boing: You can clap your hands above your head, bend your knees, and say "Boing," and the other players repeat this after you.
3. Groovilicious: You can do a funky dance and say "Groovilicious," and the other players repeat this after you.
4. Freak Out: You can yell "Freak out!" When "freak out" is yelled, all players must run to another place in the circle.

The game then continues with the person who had the last turn passing the giant imaginary ball and saying "Whoosh!"

A wit is a person who can always come up quickly with something clever to say.

Ah So Co

Six or more players

Here's a fast-paced circle game for energy, focus, and fun. Comics must always be on their toes and able to think fast because they perform live, so you never know what can happen. Play this game to build your fast-thinking skills.

The first thing you have to remember for this game is the name of the game. Practice saying it over and over: Ah So Co Ah So Co Ah So Co. The next thing you have to remember is the hand movements:

For "Ah": Put your left hand over your head with your arm in a half-circle shape and point to someone with your left pointer finger.

For "So": Put your right hand over your head with your arm in a half-circle shape and point to someone with your right pointer finger.

For "Co": Clasp both hands in front of you with your arms stretched out in front of you, and point with both pointer fingers together.

Players stand in a circle and choose one player to go first. That player says "Ah" and does the Ah movement, pointing to another player. That player says "So" and does the So hand movement, pointing to another player. That player says "Co" with the hand movement, and so on until a player is out.

How you get out:

1. If you do the wrong hand movement for a word
2. If you don't say the right word in the right order
3. If you pause too long or say "um"
4. When you are out, sit down in the circle. The game continues until there is one player left. She is the winner!

A laughingstock *is a person who provokes ridicule or seems to want people to make fun of him.*

Ork Ork

Two or more players

Remember, improvisation (improv, for short) is acting without planning in advance what will happen (see chapters 7 and 8). Some of the funniest things happen spontaneously or "in the moment." The book *Mr. Popper's Penguins* inspired this game. Through improvisation you can discover a lot about characters from books.

Two players choose a who, what, and where. *Who* is who they are in relationship to each other, such as brother and sister or teacher and student. *What* is an activity. It should be fairly active, such as building a sand castle, rather than watching television. *Where* is where the scene will take place, such as a beach or a classroom.

The two actors begin improvising their scene and acting out their who, what, and where, but in this game they can only say "Ork." How well can the players communicate to each other even though they can't use real words? Using body language, facial expressions, and attitude, Ork can mean a lot of things.

More Laughs

1. Give the players a task they must accomplish, such as baking a cake. See if they can communicate well enough, saying only Ork, to complete their task in the scene.

2. Use interpreters. Have two other players be the interpreters for the player who can only say Ork. They improvise what they think the players are trying to say, but since they don't really know, the scene can become very funny.

Laughing gas is actually nitrous oxide, a chemical your dentist might give you before pulling your tooth. It really does make you laugh.

Buy My Gibberish

Two or more players

G ibberish is a language you make up yourself. Everyone's gibberish sounds different. There are no rules and no wrong ways to speak gibberish, just let your voice do silly things and make up words as you speak nonsense. When speaking gibberish, you really have to use your body movements and facial expressions to communicate, since others cannot understand your words. This game will help you develop good movements and expressions you can use in your comic routine.

In this game, one player acts out a commercial he makes up himself, only instead of speaking English, he speaks gibberish. See if the other players can guess what the product is that he is trying to sell.

More Laughs

Create a made-up commercial with a slogan (a saying about the product, such as "Truly Tastes Great!") and a jingle (a short song about the product). But don't forget, the whole thing must be done in gibberish! For example, "Truly Tastes Great" might sound like "Booka Zoom Agaka."

Try a gibberish cooking show. See if the other players can guess what food you are preparing in gibberish.

Try a gibberish talk show. This is a real challenge because it involves more than one player. Don't plan what the subject is in advance. Have guests appear and discussions go on in gibberish. Afterward, see what the actors and other players thought the talk show was all about.

The holiday April Fools Day came about following a Mardi Gras tradition of having a feast of fools, choosing a king of the fools, and playing tricks on each other.

10

Physical Comedy

Jerry Lewis was born in 1926. His real name was Joseph Levitch. He is known for his extremely physical style of acting. He exaggerates the characters he portrays, and uses his body and facial expressions in broad ways to create humor. He was a stand-up comic before joining Dean Martin in 1946 to create a nightclub act, and later make a series of movies. He became a director and producer as well.

Physical comedy is using your body to be funny, and it often involves mishaps such as falling down or spilling something. The games in this chapter will show you how to use action as a way to create humor. **Name Writing** and **In the Pond** are physical warm-ups. (You'll find more physical and vocal warm-ups in Chapter 6.) Next, **Human Bingo** is an icebreaker, or a game that will help you get to know other players, as well as create physical comedy with them. Games like **Elbow to Elbow, Rattlesnake!,** and **Roller Coaster** will have players working together as they use their bodies in fun and interesting ways. And **What's Going On?** helps you use your body to explore your environment.

Name Writing

Any number of players

This game is a good physical warm-up because you have to use different parts of your body in funny ways.

All the players stand in a circle. Then all write their names in the air, as big as they can, with their right hands. Next, all write their names in the air with their left hands. If you are right-handed, what does it feel like to write with your other hand? Next, all write their names in the air with their right feet. Continue with other body parts, including the left foot, right elbow, left elbow, right knee, left knee, head, nose, right ear, left ear, right shoulder, left shoulder, stomach, right hip, left hip, and bottom.

A pratfall is a fake fall, with the actor often landing on his bottom in a comic way.

In the Pond

Two or more players

This is a game similar to Simon Says. One person is the leader. The other players have to listen closely to focus on and do what the leader says. If they don't, then they're out of the game. Listening and quick thinking are important skills for performers. This game helps you practice both at the same time.

Select a leader. All the other players stand and face the leader, but spread out so that there is room to move forward and back as needed. The leader gives one of four directions: in the pond, on the bank, out of the pond, or off the bank. When the leader says "in the pond," everyone must take a step forward. When the leader says "on the bank," everyone must take a step back. If you are already forward, and the leader says, "off the bank," don't move, or you're out. If you have already taken a step back and the leader says, "out of the pond," don't move, or you're out. Continue playing until only one player is left. He is the winner.

Pond humor: What did the frog say when asked how deep the pond is? Knee-deep.

Human Bingo

10 or more players

This game will help players get to know one another, or you can use it to create a theme for a party, class, or rehearsal. If you have topics you're exploring for your comic material (Chapter 2), try to fit them into this game. You can also make the game more physical by adding other actions for the players to do.

In the game Bingo you use chips to place over numbers as they are called. In this game humans become the chips.

Props

8½ × 11 sheets of paper to make the game board
Pens

Trace the game board on page 110. In each box of the table, write an instruction about things players may have in common or can do together. Here are some examples of topics to include:

- Someone who uses the same toothpaste as you
- Someone born in the same month as you
- Sing "The Itsy Bitsy Spider" with someone who signs here

- Someone who ate the same thing as you for breakfast this morning
- Someone who has the same favorite color as you
- Someone who has the same number of people in his or her family as you
- Someone who wears the same size shoe as you
- Someone wearing the same color of clothes as you
- Someone born in the same town as you
- Someone who has the same favorite television show as you
- Someone who has the same favorite food as you
- Do five jumping jacks with someone who signs here
- FREE SPACE
- Someone who has the same favorite sport as you
- Someone who can quote your favorite movie
- Someone who plays the same musical instrument (or no instrument) as you
- Someone who can sing eight words of your favorite song
- Someone who can help you name all Seven Dwarfs
- Make farm animal sounds with someone who signs here

- Someone who has read the most recent book that you have read
- Make up a secret handshake with someone who signs here
- Someone who woke up at the same time as you this morning
- Someone whose (parents') car is the same color as yours
- Someone who can spell Mississippi backward without looking
- Do the Chicken Dance with someone who signs here

Make enough copies of the game board so that each player has one. Give each player a game board. Each player walks around the room trying to find people who fit the descriptions in each of the boxes. When someone fits a description or performs an action with you, she signs or initials inside the box with the instruction that she is fulfilling.

Just as in Bingo, there are a number of ways to play and win:

1. If a player gets five signatures from five different people in a row either across, up and down, or diagonally, he shouts "Bingo!" Another player checks to make sure that the signatures are from five different people and are correct. If so, that player is the winner.
2. For a large group of people, play cover-all Bingo, which means that you must get a signature in every box in order to yell "Bingo" and win the game.
3. Another way to play is to set a time limit. When time is up, the person with the most signatures is the winner.

Notice that the space in the middle is a free space, which means it does not need a signature but still counts when making a row or full card of signatures.

Someone who uses the same toothpaste as you	Someone born in the same month as you	Sing "The Itsy Bitsy Spider" with someone who signs here	Someone who ate the same thing as you for breakfast this morning	Someone who has the same favorite color as you
Someone who has the same number of people in his or her family as you	Someone who wears the same size shoe as you	Someone wearing the same color of clothes as you	Someone born in the same town as you	Someone who has the same favorite television show as you
Someone who has the same favorite food as you	Do five jumping jacks with someone who signs here	FREE SPACE	Someone who has the same favorite sport as you	Someone who can quote your favorite movie
Someone who plays the same musical instrument (or no instrument) as you	Someone who can sing eight words of your favorite song	Someone who can help you name all Seven Dwarfs	Make farm animal sounds with someone who signs here	Someone who has read the most recent book that you have read
Make up a secret handshake with someone who signs here	Someone who woke up at the same time as you this morning	Someone whose (parents') car is the same color as yours	Someone who can spell Mississippi backward without looking	Do the Chicken Dance with someone who signs here

Elbow to Elbow

Six or more players

Sometimes making physical contact is important for characters in a play or comic routine. The way characters connect with each other tells a lot about themselves and their relationship. Body language is an important part of comedy. Directors use this game to encourage physical contact between actors. You can also use this game as a fun icebreaker or energy builder.

Choose a designated leader. All other players walk around the playing space. At some point the leader calls out "elbow to elbow!" Immediately, each player must find a partner and make his or her elbow touch the partner's elbow. After all players are connected to a partner, tell them to continue walking. Then call out another body part in the same way, such as "head to head!" Each player must immediately find a partner and make his or her head touch the partner's head. Continue the game until a number of body parts have been called.

Here's a list of the body parts you can call:

- Feet to feet
- Knee to knee
- Thumb to thumb
- Shoulder to shoulder
- Ear to ear
- Hip to hip
- Back to back

More Laughs

Play elimination **Elbow to Elbow**. The last couple to get connected is out. Continue the game until one couple is left. They are the winners!

For more of a challenge, play this game with two different body parts being called out each time. For example, call out:

- Elbow to knee (one partner's elbow must contact the other partner's knee)
- Thumb to head
- Hip to ear
- Foot to back

Rattlesnake!

In this game, players must work together to form one big snake. This game works especially well outdoors, around trees and through grass. Many comics work with a partner, such as Abbott and Costello (see Chapter 1), or in improv comedy troupes (see Chapters 7 and 8). Games like this help you work with others in unusual situations.

Props

Any objects to set up an obstacle course, such as chairs, pillows, traffic cones, and so on

Begin with everyone saying the following in rhythm (players spell out the word):

> *R-A-T (pause)*
>
> *T-L-E (pause)*
>
> *(quickly) S-N-A-K-E*
>
> *Rattlesnake!*

Practice saying it together in rhythm a number of times before you start this game.

Once everyone has the rhythm down, everyone stands in a line and holds hands. The player at the front of the line is the leader. She leads the line of people, or "snake," all over the place while everyone chants "R A T T L E S N A K E Rattlesnake!" over and over.

Make sure everyone holds hands the entire time, never letting go. The leader should lead the snake around chairs, over pillows, and up and down stairs. (If these things are not available, use other objects to set up an obstacle course for the snake to go through.) Continue the game until the snake has completed the obstacle course. If all players continue chanting together for the entire time, and never let go of their hands, they have succeeded!

Roller Coaster

Three or more players

In this game, players work together to create their own roller coaster. Comic partners and groups have to work together during the ups and downs of their routines and their audience's response. Use this game to get a feel for the wild ride of performing in a group!

All players begin by standing in a line. Players will stay in the same place for the entire game, even though they are pretending that the roller coaster moves. Pretend that you have just gotten on a roller coaster. First, put on your seat belt. Next, pretend the roller coaster begins. All players should make a jerking motion when the roller coaster first starts up. Next, pretend that you are going very slowly up a very steep hill. All players should arch their backs to show that they are moving upward. Look at the pretend amusement park below you. Wave to people on the ground. As you approach the top of the hill, you might start to act nervous or scared about going down the hill. Then, at the same time, players should quickly bend forward to show that they are going downhill. Scream, put your hands up in the air, close your eyes, or do anything that you might actually do if you were on a real roller coaster. Pretend the roller coaster makes a quick left turn. All players bend toward their left at the same time. Then make a quick right turn by bending toward your right at the same time. Have the roller coaster make a loop by arching your back, then bending forward. At the end of the ride have everyone make a jerking motion as the roller coaster comes to a stop.

You can play this as an improv game. Don't plan what the roller coaster ride will be like. Just work together and move your bodies in the same way to show that you are all riding on the same roller coaster.

More Laughs

You can also play this as a "follow the leader" or "mirror" game. Have the person in front lead the roller coaster. Everyone then does whatever the leader does. Try to do it at the same time so that no one watching will be able to tell which player is leading.

What's Going On?

Any number of players

Use your imagination in this game to become anything you want to be.

Props

Music (on tape, CD, or radio)

Select one person to be the music maker. The music maker puts on some music. All other players begin to dance around the room. After a few minutes of dancing, the music maker turns the music off. All players must freeze when the music stops. Quickly, players must think of what they could be and what could be going on based on what pose they are in. Then the music maker asks each player, one at a time, to explain what's going on. After each player has said what's going on, the music maker turns the music back on and lets the players dance until the music is stopped again. Players then freeze in a new position. Continue this game until the players have held at least three different positions.

Tip: If you are playing with a very large group of people, ask only five of them what's going on each time the music stops. Just make sure everyone has at least one turn to tell you what's going on.

Here's an example of how this game might go.

Gus is the music maker. He plays music while Kiana, Alex, and Calista dance. Gus stops the music and the other players freeze.

Gus says, "Kiana, what's going on?"

Kiana was frozen in a squatting position, so she says, "I'm a frog and I'm catching a fly."

Gus says, "Alex, what's going on?"

Alex was frozen with his hands together above his head. "I'm a basketball player and I'm shooting a basket."

Gus says, "Calista, what's going on?"

Calista was frozen with her hands on her hips. She says, "I'm angry because I have to do the dishes."

If you are playing this game by yourself, dance to some music for a few moments, then freeze in an interesting position. See if you can think about what's going on based on the pose you are in.

More Laughs

You can turn this game into a character game by expanding on **What's Going On?** Improvise or write a paragraph inspired by the pose you freeze in during the game.

Circle Games

When you're in a group and you want to laugh, try the games in this chapter. Comics and improv actors have to think quickly and be on their toes. You have to be quick in circle games such as **How Do You Like Your Neighbors?**, **Thumb Catch**, and **Kings.** Staying focused and committed to your comic characters is important. Play the focus games in this chapter, such as **Left Hand/Right Hand** and **Peepers**, to improve your focus ability. If a group of players is having a difficult time concentrating, focus games are highly recommended. But don't let the concentration part fool you. These games will still get you laughing. Speaking of laughing, if you have trouble keeping a straight face, you might want to practice playing **I Love You, Baby, but I Just Can't Smile.** Comics are not encouraged to laugh at their own jokes, so if you are in that habit, this game would be good for you. And finally, **Zoos Zeus Petals** can be played as a travel game as well as a circle game to keep you using your head.

How Do You Like Your Neighbors?

Six or more players

Listening, thinking, and responding quickly are skills that really come in handy when comics perform in front of a live audience. Here is a game where you must do all three plus warm up your body by running to your new neighbor.

Props

Chairs in a circle, 1 fewer than there are players

Choose one player to stand in the middle of the circle. All the other players sit on the chairs in a circle and count off. Each player must remember his or her number. The player in the middle should take the last number, so if there are 11 players sitting on chairs, the player in the middle is number 12.

To begin the game, the player in the middle walks up to any other player, such as number 3, and asks, "How do you like your neighbors?" Player number 3 may respond one of two ways:

1. "I like them just fine," or
2. "I do not like them at all."

If player number 3 says, "I like them just fine," the player in the middle continues asking other players, "How do you like your neighbors?" until a player responds, "I do not like them at all." If player number 3 says, "I do not like them at all," the player in the middle says, "Who would you rather have?" Player number 3 then calls out 2 numbers, such as 6 and 10. Immediately players 6 and 10 get up and go sit next to player 3. They replace the two players who were sitting next to player number 3 (players 2 and 4) who then have to run to get one of the chairs that players 6 and 10 were sitting in. Meanwhile, the player in the middle also tries to get one of the chairs that 6 and 10 used to be in and, if she succeeds, the player who does not end up with a chair is the new player in the middle. Continue the game until everyone has a turn in the middle.

Sometimes the player calling the numbers says the number of someone who is already sitting next to him. In that case, that player remains in his seat. Other times, the player calling the numbers may say the number of the person in the middle. In that case, the person in the middle takes a seat next to the person who called the number, and the others must race for the remaining seats. The important thing to remember is that the numbers who were called are guaranteed seats next to the caller, because that's who they want for their neighbors. The old neighbors and the person in the middle must race for other seats.

A comedy of manners is a satire about the customs of the wealthy.

Thumb Catch

Three or more players

Responding quickly to those around you is helpful in comedy. This game is about fast reflexes and can be played with a very large group.

Players stand in a circle and each player puts her left hand out to the left with her hand in a fist and her thumb facing down, and her right hand out to the right with her hand open and her palm up (see illustration). Your left thumb should be directly above the player to your left's palm, and your right palm should be directly beneath the player to your right's thumb.

Have someone who is not playing count to three and say "Go!" On the word "Go," all players should try to grab the thumb of the player on their right side and at the same time try to lift their own thumb fast enough so that the player on their left side doesn't grab it. Anyone whose thumb was grabbed is out and should leave the circle. Close the circle in and continue playing until there is one player left. He or she is the winner!

No matter how hard you try, you cannot tickle yourself.

Kings

Four or more players

This game combines elements from many other games. Sometimes you have to think, sometimes you have to be quick, and sometimes you just get lucky.

Props

A deck of cards

All players sit in a circle. Choose one player to go first. That player is number one. The goal of the game is to be in the number one player's spot in the circle at the end of the game.

Shuffle the cards and put them in a pile facedown in the middle of the circle. Player one picks the top card, shows it to the others, and follows the directions below. After the directions have been followed, player one places her card in another "used" pile. Player two then picks the top card, then player three, and so on until the deck has all been used. For a longer game you can shuffle the deck and go through it again.

Here are the directions for what to do when you draw a card:

- Two means "move back two." The two players before you get to move up one space to fill in your spot in the circle.
- Three means "move ahead three." The three players ahead of you move back a space.
- Four means "everyone up one," so everyone moves up one space (number one becomes the last person).
- Five means "rhyme." The player who drew the number five says a word. The next player in the circle must then say a word that rhymes with that word.

Continue around the circle until one player cannot think of a new word to rhyme with the original word. The player who cannot think of a new word goes to the last place in the circle. Everyone who was behind him in the circle moves up.

- Six and eight are "free cards." Nothing happens.
- Seven means "seven up." All players must put their hands up high. The last player to do so has to go to the end of the circle.
- Nine means "on the floor." All players must put their hands on the floor in front of them. The last player to do so has to go to the end of the circle.
- Ten means "wave." The person who drew the number 10 must start a wave by waving her arms in the air. The next person then waves his arms, and so on until the wave goes all the way around the circle. If a player is not paying attention, and doesn't wave when it's his turn, he goes to the end of the circle. (Usually no one is out on a 10.)
- Jack means "jumping jack." Everyone must stand up and do one jumping jack. The last player to do so has to go to the end of the circle.
- Queen means "category." The player who drew the queen must name a category such as cars or stores. The next player in a circle must then say something that falls into that category, such as a kind of car or the name of a store. Continue around the circle until one player cannot think of something in the category. That player goes to the last place in the circle.

- King means "king me." You get to switch places with the person who is number one.
- Ace means "ace someone." You get to send any other player to the end of the circle.

Note: Whenever a player goes to the last place in the circle, all players who were behind him (or who had a higher number) in the circle get to move up one space to fill in the circle, and make room for him at the end of the circle.

As an inside joke on Mickey Mouse, in Disney's **The Lion King,** one of the bugs that Pumba pulls out of his mouth while singing "Hakuna Matata" is wearing mouse ears.

Left Hand/ Right Hand

Six or more players

Here is a game that makes you think on your toes, which is an important skill for comedians. It's easy to learn, but difficult to play. If you are in a new group of people, this game will also help you learn everyone's name.

Everyone stands in a circle. Choose one player to stand in the middle and be the pointer. When the pointer points at you with her left hand, say your first name. When the pointer points at you with her right hand, say your favorite food. The pointer points at different people in the circle, using different hands, until someone gets out. Here's how you get out.

1. If you say your name when you were supposed to say your favorite food, or the other way around, you're out.
2. If you pause, you're out.
3. If you say "um," you're out.

It's OK if two people have the same favorite food or the same name. The game continues until everyone is out except one player. That player is the winner.

For a challenge, make sure the pointer's arms and hands look exactly the same. If the pointer is wearing a ring, or has one sleeve rolled up and the other down, it makes it easier for the players to remember which hand is which.

More Laughs

1. Try different favorites for the right hand, such as:

   - Animal
   - Band
   - Beverage
   - Color
   - Television show

2. If you are in a play, say your character's name instead of your own name when the pointer points at you with her left hand.

In Disney's Fantasia, the sorcerer's name is Yen Sid. That's "Disney" spelled backward.

Peepers

Three or more players

Usually making eye contact is a good thing, but not in this game.

All players stand in a circle very close together, with their heads down, looking at the floor. One person leads the group and says, "One, two, three, peepers!" When the leader says this, all the other players have three choices:

1. They can look at the person on their left.
2. They can look at the person on their right.
3. They can look at the person directly across from them.

If two players end up looking at each other, they are out. The people who are out leave the circle, and the others close the circle in. Continue the game until one or two players are left.

If you closely peep at Disney's animated movie **The Hunchback of Notre Dame,** *you'll see that the animators slipped in the character of Belle from* **Beauty and the Beast** *reading a book in the crowd.*

I Love You, Baby, but I Just Can't Smile

Four or more players

Did you ever wonder how comics and actors keep a straight face on stage? Did you ever have trouble trying not to laugh or smile when you weren't supposed to? Some actors think of sad things, such as a lost kitten, to keep from smiling. Others just concentrate on their character and the lines they are saying. This game lets you practice your concentration and your serious face!

Have everyone sit in a circle, and choose one player to go first. The player who is selected to go first should sit in the middle of the circle. To begin the game, the first player goes up to someone in the circle and says, "If you love me, baby, smile." The player in the circle must look him in the eyes and say, "I love you, baby, but I just can't smile," without smiling. If the player in the circle smiles, she becomes the new player in the middle, and the middle player takes her place in the circle. If she does not smile, the middle player tries again with another player in the circle until he gets someone to smile. Here are the rules.

1. You must make eye contact when saying your line.
2. The middle player may do silly things to try to get the player in the circle to smile, but he may not touch her.

Humans show their teeth when they smile, but among most mammals, showing teeth is a sign of aggression.

Zoos Zeus Petals

Two or more players

In the movie *It's a Wonderful Life*, the main character's daughter is called ZuZu. Her dad finds the petals from her flower in his pocket at an important part of the movie and cries, "Zu Zu's petals! Zu Zu's petals!" The name of this game is a play on words, or pun, taken from that phrase. This game can be played anywhere, and makes a great travel game or waiting-in-line game. When you have the room, it works great in a circle.

Everyone sits in a circle. Choose one player to go first. Starting with that player, go around the circle with everyone saying something that starts with the letter *A* that has to do with one of the following categories:

- Zoos or animals
- Zeus or mythology
- Petals or flowers

An example is aardvark (zoos) or Apollo (mythology). Continue around the circle until a player cannot think of anything. That player is then out and the next player begins with the letter *B*. The game continues until one player is left. That player is the winner. Here are the rules.

1. No repeating.
2. If there is disagreement whether or not a word fits into a category, take a vote to decide if the word is

acceptable. For example, someone might say "ants" for Zoos. There may be ants in zoos, but not as a regularly exhibited animal.

You may want to set a time limit of 30 seconds for each player to think of a word.

More Laughs

For a longer version of this game, instead of getting out when you miss, take a letter of the name Zeus for every time you miss. For example, when you miss the first time, remember that you have a Z. The second time you miss, you have an E, and so on. That way you get four chances before you're really out of the game.

*The creators of **Sesame Street** named the characters Bert and Ernie after characters in the movie **It's a Wonderful Life**.*

12

Comic Scenes for Young Actors

Previous chapters prepared you to perform comic material as a stand-up or solo performer. This chapter provides some scenes you can perform that illustrate some of the types of comedy explored in this book. *Twelfth Night* is one of Shakespeare's comedies. Included here is a scene from this play that features a jester hired to entertain a lady. For something completely different, you could leap into *Sally Ann Thunder Ann Whirlwind*, a tall tale written through improvisation by professional actors especially for children. For some real craziness, you'll find scenes from *Alice in Wonderland*, including a Mad Tea Party and a trial that looks more like a game show. A scene from *Rapunzel* has so many vegetable puns, you won't know whether to laugh or groan. And a play about *Jemima Puddle Duck* will show you some good examples of running gags. Finally, there is a list of other comedies you can find at your library or by contacting play services such as Dramatists and Samuel French.

Twelfth Night

By William Shakespeare

Humor and laughter are so important that kings and queens used to keep a jester on staff to make them laugh. Here is a scene from William Shakespeare's *Twelfth Night* that shows a jester named Feste (FES-tee) trying to make the Lady Olivia laugh.

Characters

Olivia
Feste
Servants

OLIVIA

(to servants)
Take the fool away.

FESTE

(to servants)
Do you not hear, fellows? Take away the lady.

OLIVIA

Sir, I bade them take away you.

FESTE

Misprision in the highest degree! Good Madonna, give me leave to prove you a fool.

OLIVIA

Can you do it?

FESTE

Dexterously, madam. Good Madonna, why mourn'st thou?

OLIVIA

Good fool, for my brother's death.

FESTE

I think his soul is in hell, Madonna.

OLIVIA

I know his soul is in heaven, fool.

FESTE

The more fool, Madonna, to mourn for your brother's soul, being in heaven. Take away the fool, gentlemen!

This scene is one example of Shakespeare using puns or a play on words. When Olivia tells the guards to take the fool away, she is referring to Feste, the jester. One meaning for fool is a jester or clown like Feste. However, when Feste tells the servants to take away the lady, he is implying that she is the fool for being foolish, another meaning of the word. Feste proves his point by showing Olivia, whom he calls Madonna as a praise about her virtues, that she should not be sad about her brother's death, but happy because his soul is in heaven. Thus she is a fool to be so sad.

Sally Ann Thunder Ann Whirlwind

Adapted by Emanon Theater Company

Here is a tall tale about a folk hero who could shoot lightning out of her eyes, which tickled other people. It's called a tall tale because it's larger than life or greatly exaggerated. Watch for the physical comedy, especially at the end when Davey is being tickled out of the tree. It might be funny to have an actor play the tree. The actor could hold Davey by the neck, and then be ticklish and squirmy until he lets him go at the end.

Characters

Sally
Pa
Ma
Lucy
Mike Fink
Baby Bear
Davey Crockett
Tree

SALLY

Suzette and Hurricane Whirlwind had five sons: Hail Harry, Snowy Sid, Balmy Ben, Misty Matt, and Sunny Stu. When I was born there was a thunderstorm a brewin', so my pa said:

PA

Let's name her Thunder Ann.

MA

Now, Pa, she needs a girl's name, like Sally Ann.

PA

Thunder Ann.

MA

Sally Ann.

PA

Thunder Ann!

MA

Sally Ann!

PA

Thunder Ann!

SALLY

So that's how I got my name: Sally Ann Thunder Ann Whirlwind. Now being the youngest and the only girl, I learned quick. At mealtime I always barged in and ate first. And I did my chores quick so I could go swimmin' in the river. One day I was out walkin' and I saw a girl just a sittin'.
  (to the girl)
What are you doing?

LUCY

Sittin'.

SALLY

Well, I can see that. What's your name?

LUCY

Lucy. What's yours?

SALLY

Sally Ann Thunder Ann Whirlwind. What's wrong, Lucy?

LUCY

It's Mike Fink. I love him, but he hardly even looks at me.

MIKE FINK

(walking by)
I'm hardly lookin'.

LUCY

Told ya.

SALLY

Well, here. This daisy will tell us.

LUCY

Daisies can't talk.

SALLY

Just pull off one petal and say he loves me.

LUCY

But I haven't got a bicycle.

SALLY

No! Not that kind of pedal. The petals on the flower! Here.

LUCY

(pulling a petal)
He loves me.

SALLY

(pulling a petal)
He loves you not.

LUCY

(pulling a petal)
He loves me.

SALLY

(pulling a petal)
He loves you not.

LUCY

(pulling the last petal)
He loves me!

SALLY

Well, Lucy ran off to be with Mike, and I never saw her again. Next on my travels I met a cute little baby bear. He was crying.
(to the bear)
What are you doing?

BABY BABY BEAR

Crying.

SALLY

Well, I can see that! What's wrong?

BABY BEAR

Well, first this girl came into my house and she ate all my porridge, and broke my favorite chair, and fell asleep in my bed.

SALLY

That's terrible!

BABY BEAR

Then some guy in a raccoon hat took my ma away.
(The bear cries.)

SALLY

Don't cry. We'll find your ma. Come on. Well, off we went, and before too long, we found a guy in raccoon hat with his head stuck in a tree.
(to Davey Crockett)
What are you doing?

DAVEY CROCKETT

Being stuck.

SALLY

Well, I can see that! Who are you?

DAVEY CROCKETT

I'm Davey Crockett and I can outwit, outrun, outthink, outfox, outjump anyone around!

SALLY

Well I'm Sally Ann Thunder Ann Whirlwind, and I can outwit, outrun, outthink, outfox, and outjump anyone around!

DAVEY CROCKETT

Well I'm faster than a fox.

SALLY

I'm faster than an eagle.

DAVEY CROCKETT

I'm stronger than a gorilla.

SALLY

I'm stronger than an ox.

DAVEY CROCKETT

I'm smarter than a wise old owl.

SALLY

Then how come your head's stuck in that there tree?

DAVEY CROCKETT

Oh. Uh, good question. Could you help me out?

SALLY

Only if you give this poor baby bear back his mama.

DAVEY CROCKETT

It's a deal.

SALLY

So I stared right at him until lightning bolts came out of my eyes. They tickled him so bad he started wiggling. He wiggled himself right out of that tree. The baby and his mama were reunited and Davey Crockett seemed a bit sweet on me.
(Davey makes a kissy face.)

SALLY

Yuck!

The end.

Alice in Wonderland

Here are two scenes from a humorous version of *Alice in Wonderland*. It was written through the following process: First, the actors and the director researched as many different versions of *Alice in Wonderland* as they could find. They watched many videos of different movie versions and also read a lot of books. Next, the performers brainstormed to come up with ideas about different puns and bits that would work in the play. A *bit* is a short piece of comedy that can be put into a scene without changing the course of the story line. When you *brainstorm*, everyone says all of the ideas they can think of, even if they're not sure they will work. But nobody shoots down an idea when you're brainstorming. That way everyone is free to feel creative and positive. After this, the performers spent many rehearsals improvising. They acted out scenes from the story without scripts. The director took notes and wrote down things that were especially funny that came out of these improvisations. Finally, they worked on a script that included all of their favorite things that they researched, brainstormed, and/or improvised.

Mad Tea Party Scene

Theater of the absurd is a style of theater where the comedy comes from the characters doing absurd things that would never happen in real life. The mad tea party in *Alice in Wonderland* reminded the Emanon actors of absurdist theater, so they improvised nonsense. The result is the following scene, sure to tickle your funny bone!

Characters

Alice
Mad Hatter
March Hare
Dormouse

ALICE
(to the audience)
The Cheshire cat told me I'd meet some crazy people here. These people look perfectly normal.
(Everyone does wacky things.)
Maybe not. Hello, I'm Alice.

MAD HATTER
I'm the Mad Hatter.

MARCH HARE
I'm the March Hare. Care for some tea?

MAD HATTER
Love some. Do you like riddles?

ALICE
Yes, I do.

MAD HATTER
Why is a raven like a writing desk?

ALICE

I don't know. Why is a raven like a writing desk?

MAD HATTER

I don't know.

ALICE

What kind of riddle was that?

MAD HATTER

I was hoping you would know.

ALICE

That's not a riddle at all. That's just a question.

MARCH HARE

Have you met the dormouse?

ALICE

No, I haven't.

MAD HATTER

Too bad.

MARCH HARE

Wonderful fellow.

ALICE
(pointing at sleeping dormouse)
Who's that?

MAD HATTER

Oh, that's the dormouse.

MARCH HARE

He's a counter.

MAD HATTER

A genius.

MARCH HARE

Has a way with numbers.

ALICE

I've never heard a mouse count before.

MAD HATTER

Well, wake him up.

ALICE

Yoo-hoo. Mr. Mouse, wake up.

MAD HATTER

No, no, make a sound like a cat.

ALICE

Oh. Meow!

DORMOUSE

(waking up)
Twinkle, twinkle, twinkle, twinkle.
(He goes back to sleep.)

MAD HATTER

Amazing.

MARCH HARE

Brilliant.

ALICE

That wasn't counting at all. All he said was "twinkle!"

MARCH HARE

Yes, but how many times?

MAD HATTER

Four.

ALICE

And what's a twinkle?

MARCH HARE

You don't know what a twinkle is?

MAD HATTER

Let's show her.

MAD HATTER AND MARCH HARE
(sung to the tune of "Twinkle Twinkle Little Star")
Twinkle twinkle little bat
How I wonder where you're at
Up above the world you fly
Like a tea tray in the sky
Twinkle twinkle little bat
How I wonder where you're at.

MAD HATTER

I vote the little girl tells us a story.

MARCH HARE

Good idea!

ALICE

I'm afraid I don't know any.

MAD HATTER

Too bad.

MARCH HARE

You know who tells a good tale? The dormouse.

ALICE

Let's have him tell us a story!

MAD HATTER

Good idea.

MARCH HARE

Wake him up.

ALICE

Meow!

DORMOUSE

(waking up)

What's going on?

MAD HATTER

You were telling us a story.

DORMOUSE

Oh. Once upon a time there were three sisters. No wait, that's Chekhov. Once upon a time there were three little girls. Elsie, Lacey, and Kiana. And they lived at the bottom of a well.

MARCH HARE

Well, that's a deep subject.

ALICE

What did they *eat* at the bottom of a well?

MARCH HARE

Well . . .

MAD HATTER

Well . . .

DORMOUSE

Well, they ate treacle (TRE-kle), for it was treacle well.

ALICE

What did they *do* at the bottom of the well?

MARCH HARE

Well . . .

MAD HATTER

Well . . .

DORMOUSE

Well, they drew.

ALICE

What did they draw?

MARCH HARE

Draw . . .

MAD HATTER

Draw . . .

DORMOUSE

Draw? They drew pictures of things that begin with the letter *M*. Like mice and mittens and marmalade.

MAD HATTER

M is my favorite letter, next to *N*.

MARCH HARE

And *O, P, Q* . . .

MAD HATTER

R. S. What comes after S?

ALICE

T.

MAD HATTER AND MARCH HARE

Tea? Love some!

End of scene.

Court Scene

In the book *Alice in Wonderland*, the Queen of Hearts takes Alice to court. When the Emanon players were improvising, they came up with the idea of combining the courtroom scene with a game show. This scene is the result of that funny combination and the grand ending to the show.

Characters

Alice
Queen of Hearts
White Rabbit
Mad Hatter
March Hare
Dormouse
Cook

WHITE RABBIT

Welcome to the Queen's court. All rise.
(Everyone stands.)
And now, her majesty the Queen!

QUEEN

(entering)
Where's my bow!

(Everyone bows.)
Be seated.
(to Rabbit)
Call the first witness.

WHITE RABBIT

The first witness is the Mad Hatter.
(The Mad Hatter goes to the witness booth. Everyone else cheers.)

QUEEN

State your name.

MAD HATTER

Hatter.

QUEEN

Occupation?

MAD HATTER

Hatter.

QUEEN

Well, Mr. Hatter, answer this question: Just what makes that little old ant think he can move that rubber tree plant?

MAD HATTER

Everyone knows an ant can't move a rubber tree plant.

OTHERS

Good answer!

QUEEN

Very good. I see you have high hopes. And now for the bonus question: Have you ever seen that Alice?

MAD HATTER

Confidentially speaking, she's not from around here.

QUEEN

Is there anything you'd like to add?

MAD HATTER

Add? Love to! One plus one is two, two plus two is four . . .

QUEEN

Off with your head!
 (to White Rabbit)
Call the next witness.

WHITE RABBIT

The next witness is the March Hare.
 (Hare goes to the witness booth. Everyone else cheers.)

QUEEN

State your name.

MARCH HARE

Hare.

QUEEN

Occupation?

MARCH HARE

I march, but it's June so I'm unemployed.

QUEEN

All right, Mr. Hare, how much wood would a woodchuck chuck if a woodchuck could chuck wood?

MARCH HARE

All the wood he could chuck, your majesty.

OTHERS

Good answer!

QUEEN

And now for the bonus question: Have you ever seen that Alice?

MARCH HARE

Continentally speaking, she's not from around here.

QUEEN

Tell me something I haven't heard before!

MARCH HARE

Well, a rabbit's foot really isn't lucky if you cut it off because . . .

QUEEN

Off with your head!
 (to Rabbit)
Call the next witness.

WHITE RABBIT

The next witness is the Cook.
 (Cook goes to the witness booth. Everyone else cheers.)

QUEEN

State your name.

COOK

Hal.

QUEEN

Hal what?

COOK

Hal Apenio.

QUEEN

Occupation?

COOK

I'm the cook!

QUEEN

Well, Mr. Apenio, how many licks does it take to get to the Tootsie Roll center of a Tootsie Pop?

COOK

One, two, three . . .
   (making a crunching sound)
Three!

OTHERS

Good answer!

QUEEN

And now for the bonus question: Have you ever seen that Alice?

COOK

Condimentally speaking, she's not from around here.

QUEEN

Can't you tell me anything else about her?

COOK

She needs more pepper!
   (Cook pours pepper on the Queen, making her sneeze.)

QUEEN

Off with your head!
   (to Rabbit)
Call the next witness.

WHITE RABBIT

The next witness is the Dormouse.
   (The dormouse is sleeping.)
Will someone please wake the dormouse?

ALICE

Meow!
   (The dormouse wakes up scared because he thinks there is a cat. He runs to the witness booth.)

QUEEN

State your name.

DORMOUSE

Dormouse.

QUEEN

Occupation?

DORMOUSE

Professional sleeper.

QUEEN

Answer me this: Do your ears hang low? Do they wobble to and fro? Can you tie them in a knot? Can you tie them in a bow? Can you throw them over your shoulder like a continental soldier? Do your ears hang low?

DORMOUSE

   (checking his ears)
Nope.

OTHERS

Good answer!

QUEEN

And now for the bonus question: Have you ever seen that Alice?

DORMOUSE

(to the others)
Help me out, guys!
(Others try to pantomime the answer: She's not from around here. To pantomime "here" they point to the March hare.)

DORMOUSE

She's not from around hare . . . uh . . . here!

OTHERS

Good answer!

QUEEN

Off to your bed. Well, I believe I have heard sufficient evidence to prove that the defendant, Alice, is . . .
(A bell rings.)

OTHERS

Not from around here!

QUEEN

And she is indeed guilty!

ALICE

Wait! I haven't had a chance to defend myself. I think I should be the next witness!

QUEEN

Very well.
(to Rabbit)
Call the next witness.

WHITE RABBIT

Alice.
(No one cheers.)

QUEEN

Swear her in.

WHITE RABBIT

Raise your right hand.
(Alice does.)
Raise your left hand.
(Alice does. He tickles her.)

QUEEN

State your name.

ALICE

Alice.

QUEEN

Occupation?

ALICE

I'm a little girl!

QUEEN

Tell me, Alice, what is the square root of pi?

WHITE RABBIT

A little piece of pie.

ALICE

I don't know.

QUEEN

In that case, I find you guilty!

OTHERS

Guilty!

ALICE

But all I wanted was to go home!

ALL

Oh! Well, why didn't you say so?

QUEEN

(pretending to be the good witch from The Wizard of
Oz*)*
All you need to do is click your heels three times and say,
"There's no place like home. There's no place like home."

ALICE

(clicking heels)
There's no place like home. There's no place like home. It's
not working.

MAD HATTER

(pretending to be Peter Pan)
You could fly home. All you need is some pixie dust and to
think happy thoughts.

ALICE

(closing her eyes to think happy thoughts, and trying to fly)
Hopscotch! Puppies! Candy!
(Alice opens her eyes.)
It's not working.

COOK

You could kiss this frog.
(pulls out a frog)

OTHERS

What?

COOK

Well, nothing else worked. It couldn't hurt.
(Alice kisses the frog and waits a moment. Nothing happens.)

COOK

All right, bad idea.

WHITE RABBIT

Well, why don't you just go back the way you came?
*(The White Rabbit spins her and others make it look like
she is falling up a hole. They exit, leaving Alice alone on
stage.)*

ALICE

That was some imagination!

End of scene.

Rapunzel

When writing this adaptation of *Rapunzel*, the actors took into consideration the witch's love for her garden and came up with as many vegetable puns as they could (see **Puns** in Chapter 1). *Rapunzel* is named after rampion, a type of lettuce, and in this version the witch's accomplice is appropriately a demon radish. (The puns are italicized but you'll find more fun than in just these words.)

Characters

Demon Radish
Witch

DEMON RADISH

What can I do to make you happy?

WITCH

Ah my demon radish, Rapunzel wants a friend.

DEMON RADISH

You know, I think I know how she *fields*. After all, you only made one demon radish, and if you *carrot* all for me, you'd *seed* it's not easy being *greens*. I mean, I'm in a real *pickle* here! It's *thyme* I was *raisin* some sprouts of my own, but I *cantaloupe*!

WITCH

Look, I *yam* what I *yam*, pumpkin. Between your repining and Rapunzel's whining, I'm just *plum beet*, and I need your *sage* advice!

DEMON RADISH

Oh *peas*.

WITCH

Lettuce discuss this cool as *cucumbers*. *Honeydew* you have any good ideas?

DEMON RADISH

Maybe someday a friend for me will *turnip*.

WITCH

No, and that's *fennel*.

DEMON RADISH

I think I've uncovered the *root* of all our problems, and I see the *seeds* of a solution. I'm lonely, Rapunzel's lonely—we'd make a *grape pear*!

WITCH

She hates veggies, but maybe there is a way you could help. After all, you don't want to be a vegetable your entire life. I'll turn you into some kind of pet for Rapunzel.

DEMON RADISH

But I like to talk.

WITCH

(casting spell)
I know that you fear change, dear,
But your voice will still be heard.
You can't be a demon radish,
So you'll be a talking bird.

DEMON RADISH

(now acting like a bird)
Squawk!

End of scene.

Jemima Puddle Duck

I n this scene, watch for the running gag, the joke that is repeated a number of times. Every time another character says Jemima's name, they call her by the wrong animal, such as Jemima Puddle Chicken. She corrects them by saying "duck." They think she's telling them to duck their head, so they duck down. Following the rule that the magic number in comedy is three, this running gag happens three times in this scene.

Characters

Narrator
Jemima Puddle Duck
Fox
Farm Dog

NARRATOR

Once upon a time there was a lovely dainty little lady named Jemima Puddle Duck. She watched every day as all the animals in the farm paraded around with their families. Jemima longed for a family of her own, but the farmer would never let her keep any of her eggs. Finally, Jemima got an idea. She flew off to a clearing far away and found a nice spot to lay her eggs. Just then, a very well dressed gentleman with gray whiskers approached.

FOX

Good evening.

JEMIMA

Hello. My name's Jemima.

FOX

Oh, yes, Jemima Puddle Hen.

JEMIMA

Duck.

(The fox ducks, misunderstanding her.)

FOX

What are you doing here?

JEMIMA

I'm going to lay my eggs here, so the farmer can't take them away.

FOX

Oh, no. You mustn't lay your eggs here. I have a wonderful spot for you. Walk this way.

NARRATOR

The fox led Jemima to a shack.

FOX

Make yourself comfortable. I'll be back later.

NARRATOR

Jemima laid her eggs and sat on them. In the evening she flew back to the farm. Each day she would fly to her eggs, sit on them, and fly back to the farm. Thirteen days she spent flying and sitting, flying and sitting, flying and sitting, until one day the fox came back and said to her:

FOX

Hello, Jemima Puddle Rooster.

JEMIMA

Duck.

(The fox ducks.)

FOX

I'm having a feast this evening and would like you to be the guest of honor.

JEMIMA

Oh!

FOX

Would you mind fetching some ingredients for me? I will watch your eggs while you're gone.

JEMIMA

Certainly. What do you need?

FOX

Parsley, sage, rosemary . . .

JEMIMA

She's a nice girl.

FOX

Thyme.

JEMIMA

It's four-thirty P.M.

FOX

And an onion. All the fixings for a magnificent omelette.

JEMIMA

An omelette? I wonder what an omelette is.

NARRATOR

Jemima took off to find the ingredients the fox asked for. On her way she met the farm dog.

FARM DOG

Hello Jemima Puddle Cow.

JEMIMA

Duck!

(*The dog ducks.*)

FARM DOG

Where are you going?

JEMIMA

I'm collecting some ingredients for the nice gentleman who lives over the hill.

FARM DOG

What for?

JEMIMA

Something about an omelette.

FARM DOG

He's a fox, you know.

JEMIMA

You're telling me. Well, I've got to run. Good-bye.

NARRATOR

The farm dog suspected foul play, so she followed Jemima. Jemima arrived at the shack. This time the fox was a bit short with her.

FOX

Give me those ingredients and get into that shack!

NARRATOR

He locked her in. But just then the farm dog came.

FARM DOG

Let her out!

NARRATOR

The dog chased the fox away, knocked down the door to the shack, and released Jemima.

JEMIMA

Thank you so much. Do you think you could help me carry my eggs back to the farm?

FARM DOG

Sure!

NARRATOR

So Jemima went back to her farm and was allowed to keep her eggs. And when they hatched, Jemima had the best parade of all. The end.

End of scene.

Suggestions for More Comedic Plays

Any versions of fairy tales or young people's stories adapted by Aurand Harris are great sources for comedic plays. (Mr. Harris has a wonderful way of writing scripts especially for young people to perform.)

A Doctor in Spite of Himself by Molière, a French farce with a lot of wonderfully broad characters in fantastic situations.

Scenes from *You're a Good Man, Charlie Brown*, which brings Charles Schulz's comic strip humor and characters to life.

A Midsummer Night's Dream by William Shakespeare, especially the "play within the play" of Pyramus and Thisbe, where bad actors try to act out a tragedy that ends up being more of a comedy.

Fractured Fairy Tales is a book of fairy tales adapted in funny ways for Rocky and Bullwinkle cartoons. Because they were written for television, these stories can be easily made into funny short plays.

Scenes from the play or book *Free to Be You and Me*, especially *Southpaw* and *Babies*, both two-person short scripts.

Favorite Comedy Resources

Chapter 1: Making People Laugh

Books

O'Donnell, Rosie. *Kids Are Punny: Jokes Sent to the Rosie O'Donnell Show*. Los Angeles: Warner Books, 1997.

Plays

Marx, Arthur, and Robert Fisher. *Minnie's Boys*. New York: Samuel French, Inc., [1970].

Videos

Abbott and Costello Meet Jerry Seinfeld. Universal Studios, 1994.

The Chaplin Revue. Twentieth Century Fox, 1958.

The Nutty Professor. (Starring Eddie Murphy) Universal Studios, 1996.

Chapter 2: Comic Material

Books

Scieszka, Jon. *The True Story of the Three Little Pigs*. Wrights Lane, United Kingdom: Puffin, 1996.

Plays

Harris, Aurand, adaptor, from Molière. *A Doctor in Spite of Himself*. New Orleans, LA: The Anchorage Press, Inc., 1968.

Shakespeare, William. *A Midsummer Night's Dream*. Various publishers.

Videos

Muppet Treasure Island. Jim Henson Video, 1996.

Web Sites

The Comedy Digest. www.comedydigest.com

Chapter 3: Making It Funny

Books

Carter, Judy. *Stand-Up Comedy: The Book*. New York: Dell Publishing, 1989.

Jacobs, A. J. *Fractured Fairy Tales*. New York: Bantam Books, 1999.

Videos

Bill Cosby, Himself. Twentieth Century Fox, 1981.

Chapter 4: Comic Style with Props

Videos

The Muppet Show. Jim Henson Video, 1996.

Pee-Wee's Playhouse. MGM/UA Studios, 1996.

Toy Story. Walt Disney Home Video, 1995.

Chapter 5: Comic Style with Characters

Plays

Wagner, Jane. *The Search for Signs of Intelligent Life in the Universe*. New York: Samuel French, Inc., 1991 (revised).

Videos
Aladdin. Walt Disney Home Video, 1992.

Chapter 6: Comic Style with Music

Audio Recordings
Yankovic, Weird Al. *Dare to Be Stupid*. BMI, 1985.

Videos
Royal Wedding. Warner Studios, 1951.
Vaudeville. Winstar Home Entertainment, 1997.

Web Sites
Vaudeville Memories. Personal.nbnet.nb.ca/muldrew

Chapter 7: Improv Comedy

Books
Halpern, Charna, Del Close, and Kim "Howard" Johnson. *Truth in Comedy: The Manual of Improvisation*. Colorado Springs, CO: Meriwether Publishing Ltd., 1993.
Spolin, Viola. *Improvisation for the Theatre*. Evanston, IL: Northwestern University Press, 1963.

Chapter 8: Improv Games

Books
Bany-Winters, Lisa. *On Stage: Theater Games and Activities for Kids*. Chicago: Chicago Review Press, 1997.
————. *Show Time! Music, Dance, and Drama Activities for Kids*. Chicago: Chicago Review Press, 2000.
Patinkin, Sheldon. *The Second City: Backstage at the World's Greatest Comedy Theater*. Naperville, IL: Sourcebooks, Inc., 2000.
Spolin, Viola. *Theater Games for the Classroom: A Teacher's Handbook*. Evanston, IL: Northwestern University Press, 1986.

Spolin, Viola. *Theater Games for Rehearsal: A Director's Handbook*. Evanston, IL: Northwestern University Press, 1985.

Chapter 9: Sound Silly

Videos
The Best of Andy Kaufman in Taxi. Paramount Home Video, 2000.
The Emperor's New Groove. Walt Disney Home Video, 2000.
Zoom: Best of the 70s. WGBH Boston Video, 1998.

Chapter 10: Physical Comedy

Videos
Flying Karamazov Bros. Comedy Show. M.C.E.G./Virgin Video, 1989.
The Nutty Professor. (Starring Jerry Lewis) Paramount Studio, 1963.

Chapter 11: Circle Games

Videos
Zoom: Party with Zoom. WGBH Boston Video, 1999.

Web Sites
Zoom. www.pbs.org/wgbh/zoom

Chapter 12: Comic Scenes for Young Actors

Plays
Shakespeare, William. *Twelfth Night*. Various publishers.

Videos
Alice in Wonderland. NBC-TV, 2001.

Bibliography

Banham, Martin, editor. *The Cambridge Guide to World Theatre*. London, England: Cambridge University Press, 1988.

Borgenicht, David. *Sesame Street Unpaved*. New York: CTW Hyperion, 1998.

Carter, Judy. *Stand-Up Comedy: The Book*. New York: Dell Publishing, 1989.

Givens, Bill. *Reel Gags: Jokes, Sight Gags, and Directors' Tricks from Your Favorite Films*. Los Angeles, CA: Renaissance Books, 1998.

Halpern, Charna, Del Close, and Kim "Howard" Johnson. *Truth in Comedy: The Manual of Improvisation*. Colorado Springs, CO: Meriwether Publishing Ltd., 1993.

Crystal Reference. "BioSearch." A&E Television Network. 2001 www.biography.com. 14 August 2001.

Glossary

anecdote: A short account of an interesting or humorous story.

bit: (as in a comedy bit) A short act or routine.

brainstorm: A technique of coming up with ideas by spontaneous participation in discussion or writing.

burlesque: A form of comic art characterized by ridiculous exaggeration.

canned laughter: Fake laughter often used in television sitcoms. The term originates from the device that produces the sound effect, which resembles a can.

comedy of manners: A comedy satirizing the manners and customs of a social class.

comic: A comedian.

comic relief: The comedic scene or part in an otherwise serious play, movie, book, or other work.

commedia dell'arte: Italian comedy, developed during the 16th to 18th centuries, in which masked entertainers improvised from a plot outline based on themes associated with standard characters and situations.

double take: A comic way to look surprised.

echo song: A song where a leader sings one line at a time and others repeat it.

funny bone: A part of your elbow that makes you feel a tingling sensation in your arm and hand when it's hit a certain way. Also, a sense of humor.

guffaw: A loud burst of laughter.

improvise: To perform without a script or previous preparation.

in a pickle: In an embarrassing situation.

knee slapper: A good joke that makes people laugh and slap their knee.

laughingstock: A person who provokes ridicule or seems to want people to make fun of him.

lazzi: The standard speeches or bits of business performed by comedia dell'arte characters.

mimic: To act out or imitate other characters.

monologue: A long speech said by one actor to another actor or to no one that expresses emotion and/or gives important information to move a play along.

movie trailer: A preview for a movie shown in a commercial for a movie or before a different movie in a theater.

nonsequitur: A comment that has nothing to do with what is being discussed. Some comedians use nonsequiturs as catchphrases to say when a joke doesn't go over very well.

oxymoron: A figure of speech in which opposite terms are used together (for example, jumbo shrimp).

pantomime: To perform an action without words so that you must communicate what the action is with your body and your facial expressions.

parody: A humorous imitation of something in literature, music, or art.

physical comedy: Using body movements to be funny. It often involves mishaps such as falling down or spilling something.

pratfall: A fake fall, with the person often landing on his bottom in a comic way.

project: To speak loud enough for everyone in the audience to hear and understand you. It is different from screaming.

pun: A humorous use of two words having the same or similar sounds but different meanings. The punch lines of knock-knock jokes are usually puns.

punch line: An unusual, abnormal, or exaggerated statement that is not expected and is the funny line in a joke. It is preceded by the setup.

running gag: A joke in a script or an actor's routine that is repeated a number of times.

satire: A spoof that pokes fun at something to make it look foolish or ridiculous.

scat: A style of jazz singing where the vocalist uses made-up sounds to improvise with the music.

setup: The line or lines in a joke that precede the punch line.

shtick: Someone's particular running gag or comic routine.

simile: A comparison of someone or something to an object.

sitcom: A comedy show about funny situations. The term is a combination of the words *situation* and *comedy*.

slapstick: A boisterous loud comedy, one with exaggerated characters and movements. The term comes from a paddle used in such farces and pantomimes to make a loud sound when an actor is hit by it.

spoof: (verb) To joke around about something. (noun) A kind of parody, joke, or hoax on someone or something.

stand-up comedy: A humorous performance by a solo artist or sometimes teams of artists.

stay in character: To speak and act as a specific character throughout a performance.

stitch: A pain in the back or side that can occur from laughing hard.

straight man: The serious person in a comedy duo.

swallowing your lines: Speaking a line clearly at first and then trailing off by the end of it.

theater of the absurd: Theater characterized by being senseless, illogical, contrary to common sense, or laughably foolish.

toilet humor: Humor that is in very bad taste.

vaudeville: Stage entertainment made up of acts presented by entertainers. From the French *voix de ville,* meaning "street voices."

wisecrack: A smart, obnoxious remark that can sometimes be funny.

wit: A person who can always come up quickly with something clever to say.

Index

Author Biography

Lisa Bany-Winters began performing in community plays at the age of 11. As much as she loved every aspect of theater, her favorite part was games and improvisation. She founded Emanon Theater Company when she was 15 years old and began directing and adapting children's productions based on improvisation. Within a few years, Emanon became an established professional theater company with a talented ensemble of actors who, under Lisa's direction, created original adaptations of children's classics through improvisation. Emanon performed regularly at the Halsted Theatre Centre, the Body Politic Theatre, and the Second City Northwest, and toured to countless schools, festivals, camps, and libraries throughout the Chicago area.

Her first book, *On Stage: Theater Games and Activities for Kids*, received the Parent's Choice Approval Seal for Excellence in Quality and Education and has been translated into German. Her second book, *Show Time: Music, Dance, and Drama Activities for Kids*, explores musical theater and includes activities for kids who love to sing, dance, and act. Both books are published by Chicago Review Press.

In 1998 Lisa created the Northlight Kids program (now called Northlight Theatre Academy) at Northlight Theatre, a professional Equity theater located at the North Shore Center for the Performing Arts in Skokie, Illinois. Lisa teaches acting and improvisation to students ages 8 to 17 and runs theater camps.

A graduate of Columbia College, Lisa lives in Glenview with her husband, Brian Winters, and daughter, Michaela Bany-Winters.

More Books by Lisa Bany-Winters Available from Chicago Review Press

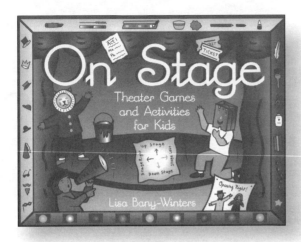

On Stage

Theater Games and Activities for Kids

- Parents' Choice Approved Seal

"A useful resource for ensemble-building games for student-run drama groups and rehearsal techniques for adult teachers/directors. . . . A terrific addition to drama collections. Purchase an extra copy for the professional shelf as well."

—*School Library Journal*

ages 6–12, 160 pages, 11 × 8½
line drawings throughout
paper, $14.95 (CAN $22.95) 1-55652-324-6

Show Time!

Music, Dance, and Drama Activities for Kids

"An introduction to musical theater. . . . Quite creative and will challenge even the more seasoned performers."

—*School Library Journal*

ages 6–12, 208 pages, 11 × 8½
line drawings throughout
paper, $14.95 (CAN $22.95) 1-55652-361-0

Both books are available at your local bookstore or by calling 1-800-888-4741.

CHICAGO REVIEW PRESS

Distributed by Independent Publishers Group
www.ipgbook.com